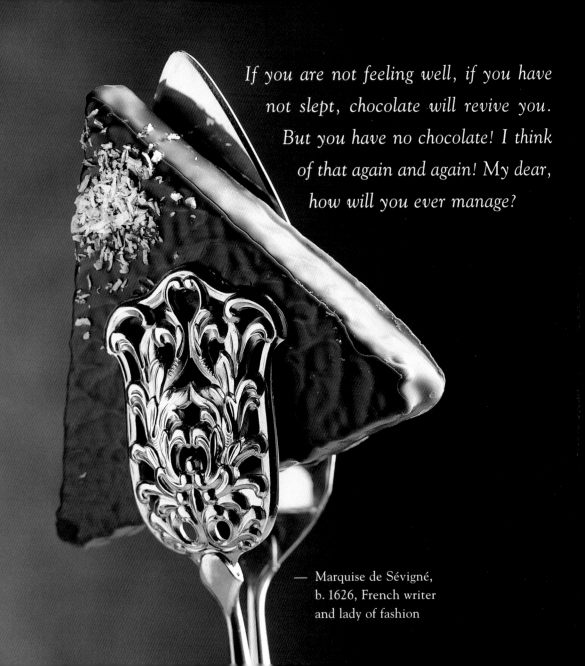

If you are not feeling well, if you have not slept, chocolate will revive you. But you have no chocolate! I think of that again and again! My dear, how will you ever manage?

— Marquise de Sévigné,
b. 1626, French writer
and lady of fashion

1,001

REASONS TO LOVE™

Chocolate

Barbara Albright & Mary Tiegreen

Stewart, Tabori & Chang
New York

Published in 2004 by
Stewart, Tabori & Chang
115 West 18th Street
New York, NY 10011

Canadian Distribution:
Canadian Manda Group
One Atlantic Avenue, Suite 105
Toronto, Ontario M6K 3E7
Canada

Library of Congress Cataloging-
in-Publication Data
Albright, Barbara.
1,001 reasons to love chocolate /
Barbara Albright & Mary Tiegreen.
p. cm.
ISBN 1-58479-329-5 (hardcover)
1. Cookery (Chocolate) 2. Chocolate.
I. Tiegreen, Mary. II. Title.
TX767.C5A42 2004
641.6'374—dc22
2004006771

Art direction by Mary Tiegreen
Designed by Dave Green/
Brightgreen Design
Photo editor: Anne Kerman

The text of this book was composed
in ITC Cheltenham Condensed,
Poppl Exquisite, ITC New
Baskerville, and Goudy.

1,001 Reasons to Love Chocolate
is a book in the 1,001 REASONS
TO LOVE™ Series.

1,001 REASONS TO LOVE™ is
a trademark of Mary Tiegreen
and Hubert Pedroli.

Printed in China

10 9 8 7 6 5 4 3 2 1

First Printing

Stewart, Tabori & Chang
is a subsidiary of

LA MARTINIÈRE
G R O U P E

Contents

—⟨⟨⟩⟩—

THE SCIENCE OF CHOCOLATE

THE LANGUAGE OF CHOCOLATE

LIFE STAGES OF CHOCOLATE

CHOCOLATE PERSONALITIES

Introduction

I am no stranger to the world of chocolate. As Editor-in-Chief at *Chocolatier Magazine* for over five years, co-author of chocolate cookbooks, a frequent judge at many, many chocolate tastings, and attendee of too many chocolate shows to count, I have viewed, touched, written about, and, most of all, *tasted* more chocolate than you can imagine. It's a tough job, but someone has to do it! And if I have learned anything over the years, it's that chocolate is a passionate subject (and that my desire for it has not diminished one bit).

No other food inspires us as much as chocolate. We offer it as a token of friendship or a gesture of love. We crave it when we want something decadent and sweet. Even the most generous among us is likely to covet a last piece of luscious luxury chocolate, or, in the case of my family, the final bite of a Marabou Milk Chocolate bar, as part of a terrific way to start the day. It makes no difference if your obsession is for dark, milk, or white, whether you prefer it solid, mixed with nuts, or filled—the desire for chocolate is unstoppable.

Mary Tiegreen and I put together a mere 1,001 of our millions of reasons to love chocolate—and it only begins to explain why we are so obsessed with the stuff. We started with the moment the Aztecs introduced Cortes to the strange, almond-shaped cocoa bean, and followed chocolate's swift journey around the world.

But this book is more than a history lesson of the world's most loved food. It's a journey into the very heart of chocolate, for chocolate is not just an item we keep in the pantry—it's part of our consciousness. A particular chocolate sweet recalled memories from childhood, brought to mind a favorite family recipe, and transported us back to a special moment in time. And most of all, what will be undeniably clear as you flip through the pages, is that there is really one reason above all others to love chocolate: chocolate does more than satisfy the sweet tooth—it satisfies the soul.

—Barbara Albright

1 There is nothing
else like it.

2 It cannot be faked.

3 It can be molded, poured, shaped, frozen, flavored, decorated, baked, dusted, whipped, and dipped in endless variations.

4 It has been considered an earthly delight for thousands of years.

5 New chocolate treats are invented every day.

6 Chocolate's botanical name – *Theobroma cacao* – means "food of the gods."

That Certain Something

7 Chocolate is a complex blend of hundreds of flavor components – nearly 2 1/2 times the amount found in simpler flavors such as lemon or strawberry.

8 Some of these flavor components (the volatiles) contribute aroma as well.

9 Chocolate's velvety, melt-in-your-mouth quality has to do with cocoa butter's melting point—97°F, just below body temperature.

10 When chocolate melts in your mouth, there is a subtle cooling sensation as the chocolate changes from solid to liquid.

11 And at the same time, a bouquet of volatiles wafts into the nasal passages through an opening in the back of the mouth.

A study conducted at the University of Pennsylvania by psychologist Paul Rozin examined the attributes of chocolate that best satisfied a chocolate craving. Volunteers were fed a real chocolate bar; a white chocolate bar that had the sweet taste of but less fragrance and none of the pharmacological ingredients of whole chocolate; and cocoa in gelatin capsules, which had none of the taste but all of the chemical properties of chocolate. Real chocolate satisfied chocolate cravings twice as well as white chocolate, but the tasteless cocoa did nothing. The experts concluded that it is the total sensory experience of eating chocolate, not just chocolate's pharmacological qualities, that satisfies a chocolate craving.

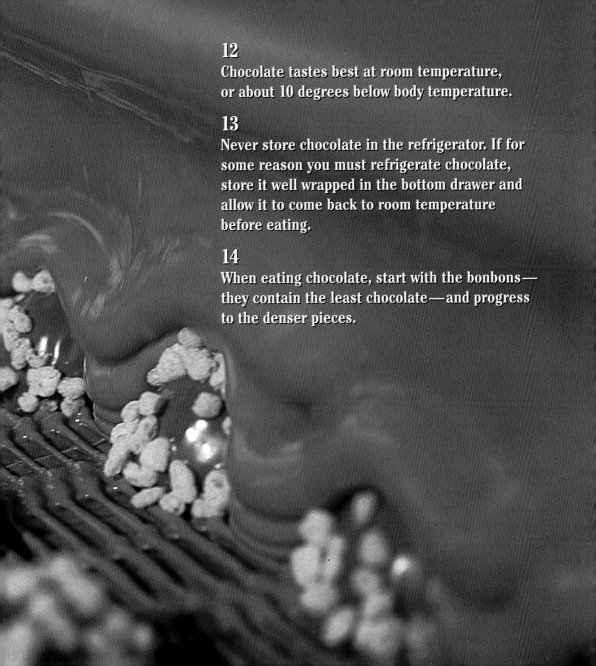

12
Chocolate tastes best at room temperature,
or about 10 degrees below body temperature.

13
Never store chocolate in the refrigerator. If for
some reason you must refrigerate chocolate,
store it well wrapped in the bottom drawer and
allow it to come back to room temperature
before eating.

14
When eating chocolate, start with the bonbons—
they contain the least chocolate—and progress
to the denser pieces.

Types of Chocolate

15 Unsweetened Chocolate

After cocoa beans have been processed and roasted, they are ground to form this purest form of chocolate. In its liquid state, unsweetened chocolate is also known as chocolate liquor (though it contains no alcohol). It must contain a minimum of 50% and a maximum of 58% cocoa butter.

16 Bittersweet, Semisweet, and Sweet Chocolate

These types of chocolate are made by combining unsweetened chocolate with sugar and flavorings such as vanilla or vanillin. They must contain at least 35% chocolate liquor. Some chocolate manufacturers today boast much higher amounts of cocoa solids and indicate this amount on the packaging. These chocolates vary widely, from manufacturer to manufacturer, depending on the amount of sugar, additional cocoa butter, milk solids, lecithin, and flavorings they contain. They are very dark brown in color.

17 Milk Chocolate

This is America's favorite eating chocolate. Milk chocolate must contain no less than 3.66% milk fat (butterfat), no less than 12% milk solids, and at least 10% chocolate liquor. Manufacturers add varying amounts of sugar, cocoa butter, lecithin, and flavorings such as vanilla and vanillin to the chocolate. The milk solids in milk chocolate make it more sensitive to heat than dark chocolate.

18 White Chocolate

This type of chocolate is a combination of cocoa butter, sugar, butterfat, milk solids, lecithin, and flavorings. It contains no chocolate liquor and gets its mild chocolate flavor and ivory color from the cocoa butter. Some products with a noticeably bright white hue have what is called confectionary or summer coating. They are made up of a mixture of vegetable fat, milk solids, sugar, lecithin, and flavorings—and no cocoa butter at all.

19 Chocolate Chips

Also called morsels and bits, they are the defining component of America's favorite cookie. The addition of lecithin and other stabilizers helps the chips hold their shape.

20 Cocoa Powder

Cocoa powder is made from chocolate liquor that has had nearly all of the cocoa butter removed by hydraulic pressure. The pressure forms what is called a press cake, which is then ground into powder. The cocoa powder available to consumers is known as breakfast cocoa and contains at least 22% cocoa butter. Dutch-processed cocoa is alkalized, which means that an alkali is added to the chocolate during processing to produce a less harsh tasting, dark cocoa. Non-alkalized cocoa powder is usually lighter in color than alkalized, but it delivers a stronger chocolate flavor. Dutch-processed cocoa powder has a milder flavor and is good for sprinkling on top of desserts and for rolling truffles in.

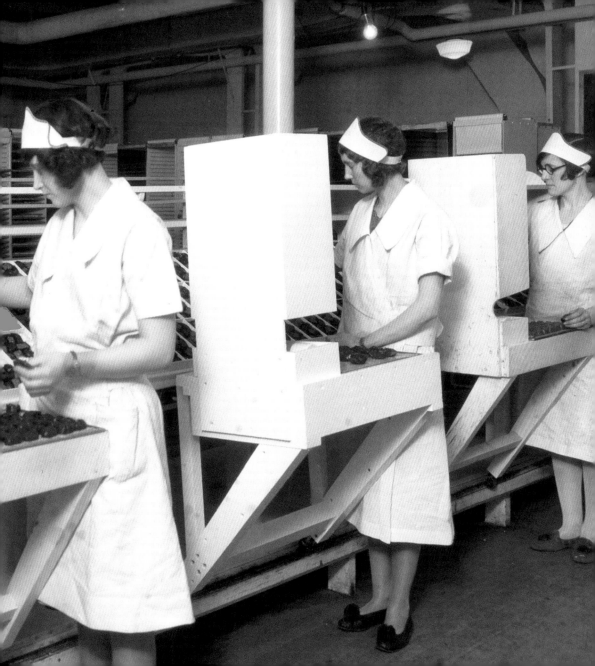

Chocolate is Good for You!

21 Chocolate and cocoa are rich sources of antioxidants, potentially beneficial compounds that may reduce the risk of heart disease, some cancers, and the effects of aging.

22 While there is a high level of stearic acid, a saturated fatty acid, in cocoa butter, it does not behave like other saturated fats and does not raise blood cholesterol.

23 A substance in chocolate inhibits the formation of dental cavities. Chocolate tends to melt away and clear quickly from the mouth, which limits the time teeth are exposed to sugar.

24 Research conducted at the University of Rhode Island suggests that chocolate milk may actually benefit individuals who are lactose intolerant.

25 Cocoa and chocolate are rich in minerals the body needs, including magnesium, iron, and copper.

26 A study of 7,841 male students at Harvard University found that those who consumed a moderate amount of chocolate and candy lived almost a year longer than those who abstained.

27 The Food and Drug Administration has exonerated chocolate as a cause of acne.

28 A recent study in Finland, published in *New Scientist* magazine, revealed that women who eat chocolate during their pregnancies have happier babies.

29
Allergies to
chocolate are
very rare.

Chocolate Myths Shattered

Numerous studies have shown that:

30
Chocolate does not cause hyperactivity.

31
Chocolate does not cause acne.

32
Chocolate does not contain a lot of caffeine.
A 1.5-ounce bar of chocolate contains only 9 milligrams of caffeine. A 5-ounce cup of coffee (depending on how it is brewed) contains 110 to 164 milligrams of caffeine. A cup of decaffeinated coffee contains 3 milligrams.

33
Chocolate does not lead to obesity,
but consuming more calories than are needed over a period of time will cause you to gain weight.

Chocolate Surveys

34

A recent survey said that 52% of American men and women
chose chocolate as their favorite flavor for desserts and sweet snacks.
There was a tie for second place, with 12% each voting for strawberry or other
berry-flavored sweets and vanilla. Cherry came in third with 3%. These
preferences hadn't changed in the 10 years since the last survey.

35

Women preferred chocolate more than men did, with 57% of women
choosing chocolate as their favorite flavor compared to 46% of men.

36

Both men and women say they prefer milk chocolate over dark chocolate
by more than a 2 to 1 margin, with 65% choosing milk chocolate
and 27% voting for dark chocolate (the remaining 8%
didn't have a favorite or were undecided).

37

The more money people make, the more likely they are
to name chocolate as their favorite flavor.

Nine out of ten people like chocolate. The tenth person always lies.

—*John Q. Tullius, artist/cartoonist*

Cravings

*A craving is defined as "intense want," "urgent need,"
and "almost uncontrollable desire." Although researchers
have tried to prove that cravings are related to certain substances
in chocolate (magnesium and phenylethylamine are two of them),
women do not report craving big bowls of leafy greens (a richer
source of magnesium than chocolate) or platters of salami
and pickled herring (both of which have higher
amounts of phenylethylamine).*

38

Chocolate is the #1 food craved by women.

39

Women report craving chocolate mostly during
the evening and late at night.

40

Women are more likely to give their chocolate-craving
children a "healthy" substitute than they are to practice
what they preach by eating that substitute themselves.

41

Women crave chocolate candy most, followed by
(in order of preference) chocolate flavorings,
toppings, and drinks.

42

69% of women surveyed report never or rarely feeling guilty when they eat chocolate.

43

65% of women surveyed report eating chocolate at least weekly.

44

15% of women surveyed report eating chocolate daily.

45

85% of women surveyed agree that, eaten in moderation, chocolate fits into a healthy lifestyle.

46

52% of women surveyed report that eating chocolate makes them happy.

—∿∿∿—

If I have chocolate around, I will eat it.
I love it, I love it, I love it.
I like a piece every day.

—Julia Louis-Dreyfus, actress

Chocolate: Tops in Antioxidants

47

The U.S. Department of Agriculture and the Journal of the American Chemical Society have ranked the top antioxidant foods based on ORAC (Oxygen Radical Absorbance Capacity), which is a measure of the ability of foods to subdue harmful oxygen-free radicals that can damage our bodies.

Dark chocolate came in first, with 13,120 ORAC units per 100 grams of chocolate. Next was milk chocolate, with 6,740 units. Prunes came in third (5,770 units), followed by raisins (2,830 units). These findings make a compelling case for the health benefits of chocolate-covered raisins, not to mention a good reason to introduce chocolate-covered prunes to the health-food market.

Magic Beans

*There are 3 main varieties of cocoa beans grown and harvested for our chocolate pleasur
They are classified into 2 types, the "flavor" beans and the "bulk or ordinary" beans.*

48
Criollo

Criollo trees (the word means "native") are a delicate variety that requires very specifi
soil and climate conditions. The beans from these trees deliver an outstanding flavor
but make up only about 2% of the crop because of their fragility. Grown in Mexico,
this variety undoubtedly was used to make the chocolate drink enjoyed by Montezuma.
These beans dominated the market until the middle of the 18th century.

49
Forastero

These are hardy cocoa trees (the word means "foreign") that produce strong,
astringent beans and make up about 90% of the crop. This group of trees
contains cultivated, semi-wild, and wild varieties.

Large areas of Brazil and West Africa are planted with Amelonado varieties including
Comum in Brazil; West African Amelonado in Africa; Cacao Nacional in Ecuador; and
Matina or Ceylan in Costa Rica and Mexico.

50
Trinitario

Trinitario cocoa trees are a cross between the Criollo and the Forastero, and cultivatio
of these flavorful beans spread to Venezuela and then to Ecuador, Cameroon, Samoa,
Sri Lanka, Java, and Papua New Guinea.

51
Cacao seeds are called *pepe de oro*, "seeds of gold," in Ecuador.

52
Most cacao is now produced in the sunny tropical climate of Africa.

53
Hawaii has only recently begun to grow chocolate. All five types of the insects needed to pollinate the minute flowers to form mature cocoa pods can be found in Hawaii. In Hawaii, cacao trees produce up to 25 pods per tree—elsewhere, five pods at most will form on a tree.

Coffee and Chocolate

❧

*Coffee and chocolate are frequently grown
in the same areas of the world, and they compliment
each other perfectly. The vanilla bean is another natural partner
with these beans. Interestingly, coffee and chocolate preferences
tend to be regional—for instance, in the San Francisco area
coffee drinkers tend to like espresso roast coffees
and they also like their chocolate to be deep,
dark, and stronger.*

54
Mochaccinos

55
Mocha Frappuccinos®

56
Brownie Frappuccinos

57
Peppermint-mocha coffee

58
Sprinkling extra cocoa powder on your coffee

59
Chocolate-covered espresso beans

Chocolate Geography

60

Cacao trees grow only within 20 degrees of the equator.

61

Cacao is grown in at least 33 countries within this equatorial band:

Mexico	Togo
Costa Rica	Nigeria
Panama	Cameroon
Jamaica	Equatorial Guinea
Cuba	Gabon
Haiti	Bioka
Dominican Republic	São Tomé
Grenada	Congo
Trinidad and Tobago	Sri Lanka
Venezuela	Malaysia
Colombia	Lebanon
Ecuador	Indonesia
Peru	Philippines
Brazil	Papua New Guinea
Sierra Leone	Fiji Islands
Ivory Coast	Samoa
Ghana	

Chocolate History

62

More than 2,000 years ago, the Mayan Indians created a ritual beverage made from ground cacao beans mixed with water, black pepper, vanilla, and spices. The beverage was shared during betrothal and marriage ceremonies, perhaps one of the earliest links between chocolate and romance.

63

The ancient Mayans used cacao beans as currency; they were only consumed when they wore out. Ancient records show that a horse could be purchased for 10 beans. Heroes were rewarded with chocolate.

64

The Spanish kept cacao a secret from the rest of the world for nearly 100 years, until some Spanish monks leaked the secret of *xocolatl*.

65

The ancient Toltecs of Central America thought so much of cacao that when they burned incense before the altars of their gods they included a cocoa branch.

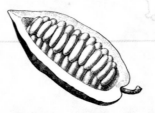

66

By the mid 1600s, chocolate as a beverage had gained
widespread popularity in France—it was praised
as a delicious, health-giving food and was mostly
enjoyed by the wealthy. One visionary Frenchman
opened the first hot chocolate shop in London,
and by the 1700s these "chocolate houses"
had become popular in England.

67

The steam engine was produced
during this century, which mechanized the grinding
of cocoa beans and lowered production costs,
making chocolate more readily available.

68

The first chocolate bar, made of chocolate,
extra cocoa butter, and sugar was produced
in England by Fry and Sons in 1847.

69

The first "chocolate box" was introduced by
Richard Cadbury in 1868, a candy box he decorated
with a painting of his young daughter holding
a kitten in her arms.

Chocolate Geology

70
The Chocolate River
of the Upper Peninsula of Michigan,
runs north and northeast, emptying
into Lake Superior.

71
The Chocolate Drops
a spectacular stand of ancient rock
in Canyonlands National Park
in Moab, Utah

72
The Chocolate Mountains
in eastern Imperial County
near Brawley, California

73
The Chocolate Pots
in Yellowstone Park, these unusual
3- to 4- feet-high cones sport a rich,
chocolate hue with colorful streaks
and a nice, hot 130-degree
average temperature.

74
Chocolate Fondue

Pull out all the stops and serve lots of interesting, cut-up fruits and cakes with this chocolate dip. Fondue gets your guests involved as they take the plunge, making it a perfect party dessert.

2/3 cup light corn syrup
1/2 cup heavy (whipping) cream
8 ounces semisweet or bittersweet chocolate
1/4 teaspoon vanilla extract
Cut-up fresh fruit, cookies, pretzels, and pound cake for dipping

Place the corn syrup and cream in a large microwavable bowl and microwave on High for 1 1/2 minutes, or until the mixture comes to a boil. Add the chocolate and vanilla and stir until completely melted.

Pour into a fondue pot and keep warm. Serve with the fresh fruit, cookies, pretzels, and pound cake

Makes 12 servings

The Language of Chocolate

*Chocolate has such complexity of flavor, texture, and aroma
that describing it is as much of a challenge — and an art — as it is for wine.
Connoisseurs and chocolatiers have developed a special vocabulary to express
chocolate's infinite variety, as well as its potential shortcomings.*

75
Mouthfeel

Mouthfeel involves the entire physical and chemical interaction of a food
in the mouth, from the initial perception on the palate from the tip of the tongue
to the back of the throat, to the first bite, through chewing to swallowing. High quality
chocolate should be both smooth and creamy and melt right away, with a slightly
cool quality because of the low melting point of cocoa butter.

Manufacturing Lingo

76
Bloom

Gray-white blotches that develop on chocolate
that is not stored correctly. There are two types
of bloom: Sugar bloom occurs when the chocolate has
been stored in damp conditions, causing moisture to
collect on the surface. As the moisture evaporates,
small crystals of sugar leach out of the chocolate and
leave the surface feeling rough. Fat bloom occurs
when the chocolate gets too warm. Stable cocoa
butter crystals melt and reform as unstable
crystals. While the chocolate may look
unsightly, it is still safe to eat.

77
Ballotin

The long deep boxes that chocolates
are packed in.

78
Conching

A process that involves kneading the ground
cocoa beans with special heavy rollers, which
develops the flavor of the chocolate.

79
Temper

To alternately heat and cool chocolate to specified temperatures, which stabilizes the product so that it is smooth and glossy and holds its shape.

80
Couverture
High-quality chocolate that contains a minimum of 32% cocoa butter, which enables it to form a much thinner shell than ordinary confectionary coating. Couverture is used to form the shells of fancy chocolates.

81
Enrobe
To coat a filling with a thin layer of chocolate. Many popular American candy bars are enrobed in chocolate.

82
Ganache
A mixture of chocolate and heavy cream frequently used to fill and frost cakes and other desserts. It is also used as a filling for truffles.

83
Gianduja
A beloved Italian confection made with chocolate and hazelnuts. It's used as a filling for chocolates and to create other desserts.

84
Nibs
The meat of the cacao bean from which chocolate is made. These are the dark rich bits that detach themselves from the beans after they have been roasted.

85
Palet
A round thin wafer of chocolate.

86
Pavé
A square chocolate with rounded corners —a popular shape for high-end French-style chocolates.

Making chocolate-coated candies constituted the largest part of the candy-making activity at the Loft factory. Most of the centers—creams, caramels, jellies—would be cooked in kettles and while still soft poured into starch molds for shaping and stiffening. Nuts and hard candy would skip the starch process because they could be coated directly.

The candy maker would cook up a 90- to-100-pound batch of a given center in a given color and flavor (say, raspberry creams). At the same time, on the floor below, the starch trays were being filled with starch and stacked at the end of the starch conveyor. (The starch tray was a wooden tray about 12 by 4 inches with a 2-inch lip around all 4 sides.) The candy maker on the floor above would open the spigot at the bottom of the kettle, allowing the batch to move through a pipe to a pump positioned over the conveyor. The trays would move along the conveyor, and as each one passed under a matrix (a die), the matrix would be pushed down into the starch and make a number of impressions in the starch of the desired shape and size. The tray would then move under the pump, which would squirt the proper amount of the center into each impression. The filled trays would then be stacked and stored for a day or so until they set.

When a particular center was needed, those trays would be brought to another conveyor. Mechanical arms would pick up each tray, upend it, and give it a good shaking. The starch and its contents would fall out onto a shaking mesh conveyor. The starch would fall through the mesh and the centers would move along to the enrobers for coating. Since the starch is tasteless and odorless, any small amount stuck to a center wouldn't be noticeable.

—Samuel R. Kostick, former Vice President, Loft Candy

Tastings

All chocolate starts with cocoa beans—the type of chocolate varies depending on how the beans are roasted and processed. When cooking with chocolate, you should use the specific chocolate that is called for in the recipe. Take note of the appearance, snap, aroma/flavor, and mouthfeel/texture. For instance, a chocolate that is glossy rather than dull is preferable, and the chocolate shouldn't be crumbly. It should break with a clean snap. As you taste the chocolate, you will develop your own personal "taste library" of qualities that will help you pinpoint what it is you like about a particular chocolate.

87 Appearance

Fine chocolate should be rich and even in color with a smooth, glossy surface. Cracked or dull-colored chocolate is an indication of poor quality.

88 Aroma

It should be fragrant with a strong chocolate aroma.

89 Snap

High quality chocolate should break cleanly; it should not be crumbly, powdery, or dry.

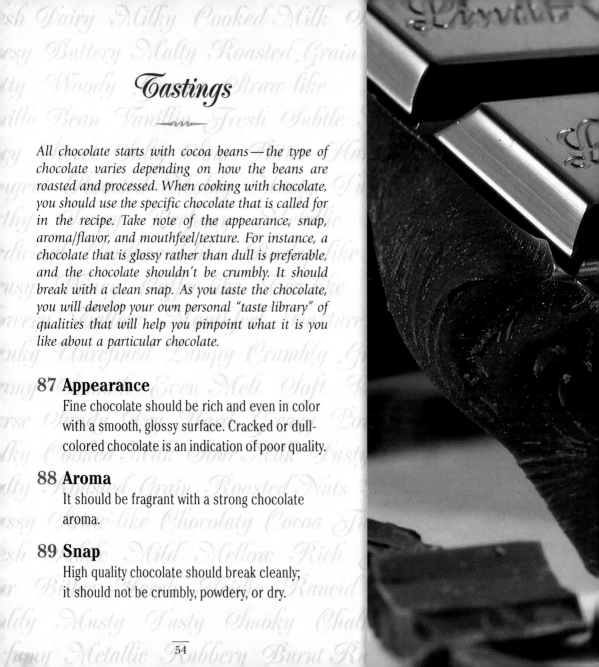

90 Texture

Fine chocolate should feel smooth and melt evenly in your mouth, without lumps. It should not be gritty, grainy, waxy, sticky, or chewy.

91 Overall Flavor

It should taste rich, full-bodied, and chocolaty.

92 Finish (aftertaste)

The chocolate should leave a pleasant, mellow taste in the mouth; it should not be acidic, sharp, or cloying.

*Strength is the capacity
to break a chocolate bar
into four pieces with
your bare hands—
and then eat just one
of the pieces.*

—Judith Viorst, author

Great Words to Describe Chocolate

93 **Fudgy**

94 Sublime

95 *Seductive*

96 **Indulgent**

97 ***Gooey***

98 **Nut-filled**

99 *Cream-filled*

100 **Mouth-watering**

101 *Decadent*

102 *Heavenly*

103 Tempting

104 **𝔚𝔦𝔠𝔨𝔢𝔡**

105 *Bliss*

Chocolate Taster's Lexicon

These words are are a sampling of what experienced tasters
frequently use to describe chocolate.

AROMA/FLAVOR

106 Sweet	118 Smoky	130 Like cardboard
107 Salty	119 Chalky	131 Like burlap
108 Sour	120 Earthy	132 Like rubber
109 Bitter	121 Dirty	133 Like burnt rubber
110 Mild	122 **Cheesy**	134 Grains (roasted)
111 Mellow	123 **Buttery**	135 Nuts (roasted)
112 Subtle	124 **Caramel**	136 Milk (cooked)
113 Fresh	125 **Malt**	137 Milk (sour)
114 Musty	126 Rich	138 **Chocolatey**
115 Dusty	127 Flat	139 **Cocoa**
116 Moldy	128 Spicy	140 **Fudgy**
117 Nutty	129 Woody	141 **Vanilla**

MOUTHFEEL/TEXTURE

166 *Melting*	174 **Chunky**	182 **Powdery**
167 *Soft*	175 **Chalky**	183 **Waxy**
168 *Velvety*	176 **Crumbly**	184 **Coarse**
169 *Smooth*	177 **Lumpy**	185 **Sandy**
170 **Fatty**	178 **Grainy**	186 Dry
171 **Sticky**	179 **Greasy**	187 Hard
172 **Creamy**	180 **Gritty**	188 Snap
173 **Chewy**	181 **Gummy**	189 Crack

By Any Name

It tastes just as good.

190
Schokolade
(German)

191
Cioccolato
(Italian)

192
Chocolade
(Dutch)

193
Chokolade
(Danish)

194
Sjokolade
(Norwegian)

195
Choklad
(Swedish)

196
Czekolada
(Polish)

197
Шоколад
(Russian)

198
Σοκολάτα
(Greek)

199
초콜렛
(Korean)

200
チョコレート
(Japanese)

201
巧克力
(Chinese)

202
Cokelat
(Indonesian)

203
Kokoleka
(Hawai'ian)

204
Cacahuatl
(Nahuatl)

205
Chocolat
(French)

**206 Wearing it well
(on your hands and face)**

Childhood Chocolate

Lucky chocophiles can remember their first taste of chocolate almost as perfectly as their most recent. It's still wonderful.

—◦/◦/◦—

207 Licking the beaters and bowl after your mom has made chocolate frosting

208 Buying a frozen chocolate treat from the ice cream man on a hot summer day after Little League baseball

209 Fudgsicles, and sporting a drippy chocolate mustache afterward

210 Catching chocolate ice cream as it drips down the side of an ice cream cone, and if you are brave, biting off the point of a sugar cone and slurping out the dripping ice cream

211 Adding chocolate sprinkles to an ice cream treat

212 Being rewarded with a hot fudge sundae for getting straight A's

213 Drinking Hershey's Syrup out of the bottle when your mom isn't around

214 The chocolate Kiss your mom packs in your lunchbox to let you know that she cares

215 Discovering that your mom included a Snickers bar for dessert in your lunch box instead of a piece of fruit

216 Going to the Dairy Queen after winning a swim meet or softball game for a Buster Bar: a chocolate-coated cylindrical ice cream bar with layers of fudge sauce and peanuts alternating with vanilla ice cream

217 Chocolate-dipped soft serve ice cream cones

218 Drumsticks, with all their contrasting textures

219 Ice cream sandwiches such as Klondikes and Chipwiches

220 Ice cream bars such as Heath Bar Crunch, DQ Dilly Bars, and Dove B

221 Frozen chocolate bars at the swimming pool

222 Chocolate-covered frozen banana

223 The chewy chocolate center of a Tootsie Roll Pop

224 Counting the number of licks it takes to get to the center of a Tootsie Roll Pop

225 Burning your tongue on hot cocoa after ice skating because it tastes too good to wait for it to cool

226 Serving hot chocolate in your bran new pink "tea set"

227 Hot cocoa mustaches

228
Sipping hot chocolate with
marshmallows after spending
the day building a snowman

229 When you get to pack your own lunch box and you fill it full with Hershey's Kisses

230 Chocolate cake and milk as an after-school snack

231 Making chocolate chip cookies with your mom, your boyfriend or girlfriend, and then with your own children

232 Selling chocolate as a school or community fundraiser

233 Walking around town with your best friend and a 2-pound bag of M&M's as you discuss life

234 The delicious European chocolate bars that your father brought back from his fishing trip to Canada

235 Original Nestlé® Toll House Chocolate Chip Cookies

Whether it's the first time you are making a batch of chocolate chip cookies, or the hundredth, these are always a welcome treat. Bakers have been known to eat all the dough before a single cookie can get to the oven.

2 1/4 cups all-purpose flour
1 teaspoon baking soda
1 teaspoon salt
1 cup (2 sticks) unsalted butter, softened
3/4 cup granulated sugar
3/4 cup packed brown sugar

1 teaspoon vanilla extract
2 large eggs
2 cups (12-ounce package) Nestlé Toll House Semi-Sweet Chocolate Morsels
1 cup chopped nuts

Preheat oven to 375°F.

Combine the flour, baking soda and salt in a small bowl. Place the butter, granulated sugar, brown sugar, and vanilla in a large mixing bowl and beat until creamy. Add the eggs, 1 at a time, beating well after each addition. Gradually beat in the flour mixture. Stir in the morsels and nuts. Drop by the rounded tablespoon onto ungreased baking sheets.

Bake for 9 to 11 minutes, or until golden brown. Cool on the baking sheets for 2 minutes, then remove to wire racks to cool completely.

Makes about 5 dozen cookies

236
Having a child who
wants to trick-or-treat
but doesn't like candy

halloween

237
More money is spent on chocolate candy for Halloween than for any of the other major chocolate holidays—Easter, Christmas, or Valentine's Day.

238
Trick-or-treating at the home of people who give out full-sized chocolate bars

239
Investigating your children's trick-or-treat bags and selecting your favorite types of chocolate candy

Educational Chocolate

—◦◦◦—

*Teachers across the country have realized that chocolate makes a great
learning tool — kids love to learn about a food they love!*

240
Chocolate Math

There's probably no better way to hold a child's attention during arithmetic
lessons than counting M&M's, adding and subtracting Hershey's Kisses,
and multiplying and dividing Hershey's Milk Chocolate bars.
And for each operation, there's a book!

241
The Great Chocolate Experience

A delicious internet-based learning project designed to help
third-graders learn estimating, charting, graphing, predicting probability,
and other math skills by combining M&M's, math, and hungry kids. Students in
the United States and Canada analyze fun-size bags of M&M's to determine
packaging patterns based on number, color, and geographic region.

242
A Chocolate Curriculum

Designed to help teachers integrate the history and properties
of chocolate into standard social studies and science courses
as a way of making learning meaningful and fun.

JIMMY NELSON with DANNY O'DAY and FARFEL

243 Farfel the Dog

Children of the 1950s and 60s will remember Farfel, the friendly, floppy-eared dog that appeared in Nestlé commercials along with his owner, Danny O'Day, and their puppeteer, Jimmy Nelson. The trio were regulars on the Ed Sullivan show, and made frequent appearances on the Texaco Star Theater, starring Milton Berle, before the Nestlé Company hired them in 1955 to promote Nestlé's Quik chocolate drink.

In the classic TV spot, Nelson remarks, "It's time to recharge with delicious Nestlé's Quik." After the Nestlé's jingle plays "N-E-S-T-L-E-S ... Nestlé's makes the very best," Farfel, in an extended yawn, delivers the line "Chaw-Clat." As with many great TV moments, the signature snapping shut of Farfel's jaw after saying "Chaw-Clat" was an accident. Nelson's hand slipped inside the puppet during rehearsal, causing Farfel's jaw to clap shut. The powers-that-be at Nestlé loved it, and the rest is broadcast history.

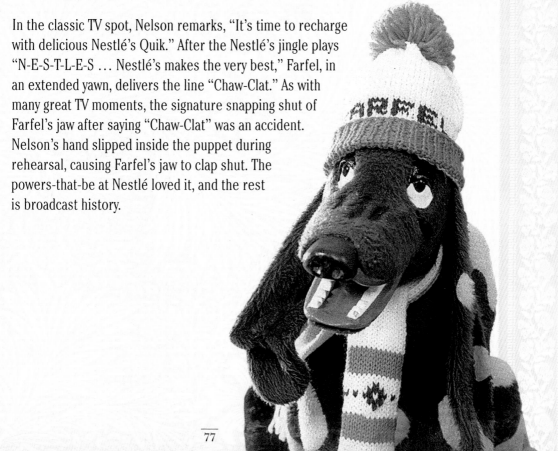

244 Chocolate Egg Cream

Here is a Big Apple favorite. Stand back when you add the seltzer and prepare to enjoy a perfect thirst quencher on a hot summer day.

1 cup cold milk
3 tablespoons chocolate syrup, homemade (see page 171)
  or store-bought
1/2 to 3/4 cup seltzer, well chilled

Place a large glass in the sink. Pour the milk and chocolate syrup into the glass and stir to combine.

Pour the seltzer into the glass, creating a foamy head.

Makes 1 serving

245 Classic Chocolate Shake

Store some glasses in the freezer so you will always have frosted glasses on hand to serve this and other cold beverages. For a thinner shake, add a little more milk.

1 cup chocolate ice cream
1/4 cup cold milk

Combine the ice cream and milk in the container of a blender and process just until smooth. Pour into a chilled glass and serve immediately with a straw and a spoon.

Makes 1 serving

246 It's a great get-well present

Chocolate Relationships

247 It's something you and your teenage daughter can agree on

248 It doesn't talk back

249 It's dependable

250 It'll be waiting for you when the going gets tough

251 It's a peace offering

252 One size fits all

253 It's cheaper than therapy

254 Finding chocolates on the pillow
of your bed at a fine hotel

Midlife Chocolate

255
Discovering dark chocolate
(73% of consumers between the ages
of 45 and 54 prefer dark chocolate)

256
Feeling smug about the fact
that the cocoa butter in chocolate
does not raise your blood cholesterol

257
When the checker at the supermarket
hands you your chocolate purchase
instead of bagging it

258
As a reward for having your teeth cleaned

259
As a reward for losing 2 pounds
on your diet

260 Setting out the very best chocolates, along with the very best cognac, for a special night

261 Smearing melted chocolate ... somewhere

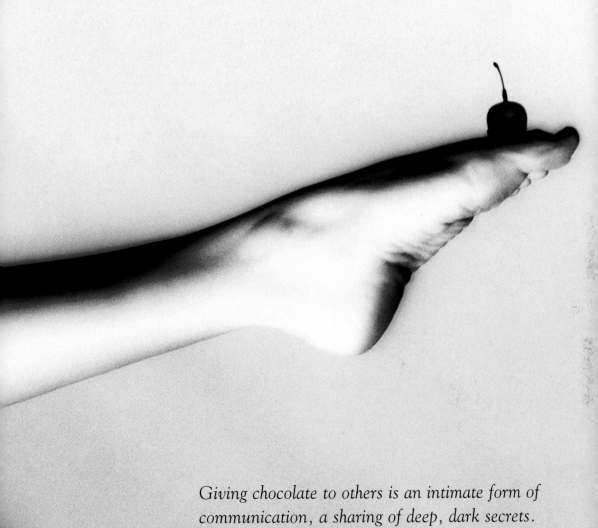

Giving chocolate to others is an intimate form of communication, a sharing of deep, dark secrets.

——Milton Zelman, publisher of *Chocolate News*

262 You are never too
tired to eat chocolate.

Why Chocolate Is Better Than Sex

263
Having chocolate doesn't keep your neighbors awake.

264
You are never too young or too old for chocolate.

265
Good chocolate is not hard to find.

266
You can ask a stranger for chocolate without getting your face slapped.

267
You can have chocolate on top of your desk during office hours without upsetting your co-workers.

268
The word "commitment" doesn't scare off chocolate.

269
You can make chocolate last as long as you want it to.

270
You can safely have chocolate while you are driving.

271
You can get chocolate.

Valentine's Day

The fourth biggest chocolate holiday of the year.

—◦◦◦—

272
Sales of boxed chocolates are higher on February 14th
than any other day of the year.

273
In the United States 36 million heart-shaped boxes of chocolate
are produced for Valentine's Day.

274
Americans spend over $1 billion on candy each Valentine's Day.
68% of American men age 50 or older say they'd prefer receiving chocolate
over flowers from their sweetheart on Valentine's Day.

275
The first Valentine's Day candy box was introduced
by Richard Cadbury.

276

The first Valentine's Day that your mom and dad gave you
your very own heart-shaped box of chocolates.

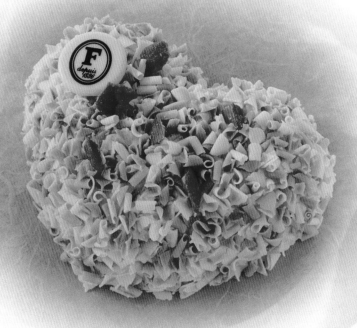

277

Using your Valentine's Day chocolate box long after the chocolate is gone
to hold letters and mementos. Years later, the aroma of chocolate
still greets you each time you open the box.

278
Casanova
claimed he drank chocolate
instead of champagne.

Red Hot Chocolate Lovers

279
Princess Maria Theresa of Spain
helped introduce chocolate to France when she presented
cocoa beans as an engagement present to Louis XIV.
She was passionate about both the king and chocolate.

280
Contesse du Barry
famous mistress of Louis XV, was purported
to "ply her lovers with chocolate to whip up
their ardor in gratifying her lust."

281
Montezuma II
served his cacao mixture to his harem
as the royal love potion.

*All I really need is love,
but a little chocolate now
and then doesn't hurt!*

—Lucy Van Pelt, in *Peanuts*,
by Charles M. Schultz

EN VENTE ICI
Praslines Mazet
DE MONTARGIS

Love and Chocolate Conquer All

In 1907, Francesco Buitoni and Annibale Spagnoli jointly established the Perugina company, originally as a small wedding cake manufacturer. In 1922, Francesco Buitoni's 20-year-old grandson, Giovanni Buitoni, was working for Perugina in the marketing department and Luisa Spagnoli, the wife of Annibale, was working in the technical division, creating the original recipes for the company's candies. Even though Luisa was married and about 20 years older than Giovanni, the two of them fell madly in love. During the work day, they were only able to communicate with each other via written messages tucked into the new products that Luisa developed and passed along to Giovanni for his inspection.

Chocolate and Wine

There are few pairings as romantic as chocolate and wine.

282
Chocolate Dipped Wine

Full-sized bottles of Moet & Chandon White Star Champagne, Dom Perignon, Beringer White Zinfandel, J. Lohr Cabernet, or J. Lohr Riverstone Chardonnay, dipped in fine gourmet Guittard dark chocolate. A simple pull of the ribbon "zipper" on the outside releases the chocolate covering so the two can be enjoyed together.

283
Raspberry Pinot Noir
Chocolate Sauce

284
Coffee Merlot
Chocolate Sauce

285
Chocolate Zinfandel
Sauce

286
Chocolate Cabernet
Sauce

287
Chocolate Port Sauce

288
Chocolate Brandy
Sauce

289
Chocolate Amaretto
Sauce

290
Chocolate-Coffee
Sauce with a hint
of Kahlua

291
Chocolate-Orange
Sauce with a hint of
Grand Marnier

292
Chocolate-Raspberry
Sauce with a hint
of Chambord

Chocolate Personalities

293
Quetzalcoatl

God of wisdom and knowledge, gave chocolate to the Aztec people.

294
Montezuma II

The last great Aztec emperor had vast storehouses of cocoa beans. He served great golden goblets of the royal beverage to his Spanish visitors.

295
Hernándo Cortés

In 1519, the Spanish explorer tasted a drink made by the Aztecs, called *cacahnuatt*. He took some cacao beans back to Spain, where a similar drink was concocted with sugar and heated, creating the first known cup of hot cocoa.

296
Thomas Jefferson
was a big fan of hot chocolate.
He hoped it would someday take
the place of coffee and tea.

Famous and Talented

—◦◦◦—

297
Alfredo "Chocolate" Amenteros
Important trumpet player, in the Afro-Cuban style,
of the second half of the 20th century.

298
Ethel Mars
Candy heiress, owned a thoroughbred racehorse
stable named Milky Way Stables in the 1930s.
Her prizewinning filly, Forever Yours,
was named after a popular candy
bar of the time.

—◦◦◦—

*Chocolate is the greatest gift
to women ever created, next to
the likes of Paul Newman and
Gene Kelly. It's something
that should be had
on a daily basis.*

—Sandra Bullock, actress

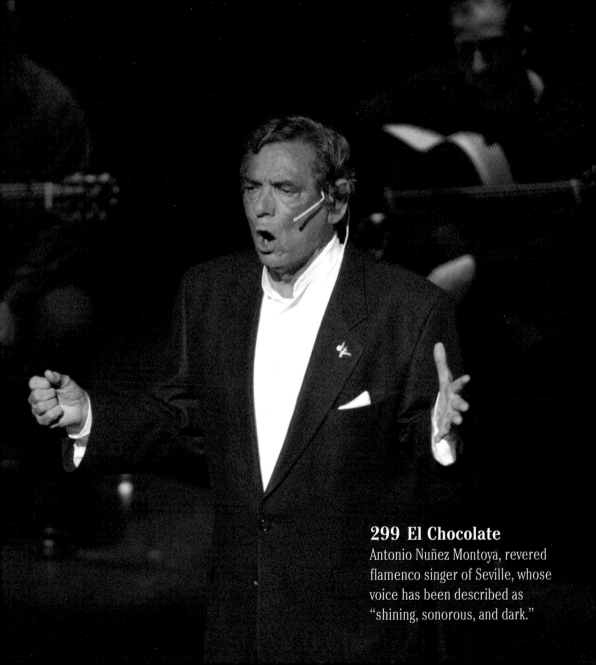

299 El Chocolate

Antonio Nuñez Montoya, revered
flamenco singer of Seville, whose
voice has been described as
"shining, sonorous, and dark."

Zips Chocolate Chip's Chocolate Offspring

Chips Hot Chocolate and Rich N Chocolatey may be the most famous of Chip's name-lucky offspring, but when it comes to chocolate-filled names, it's a family affair.

300 Chocolate Tigress

301 Aflair of Chocolate

302 Chip Chocoholic

303 Im Chocolate Flowing

304 Jazzy Chocolate

305 Chocolate Raisinette

306 Thoroughly Chocolate

307 Tales of Chocolate

308 Chocolate Chip Cooky

309 Chocolate Topper

310 Chocolate Springtime

311 Chocolate Ribbons

312 Promise Me Chocolate

313 Dark Chocolate Chip

314 Chocolate Chiplette

315 Time For Chocolate

Rich N Chocolatey

316
Zips Chocolate Chip
A champion quarter horse stallion from
Myers Horse Farm of Ashland, Ohio.

What you see before you,
my friend, is the result of
a lifetime of chocolate.

—Katherine Hepburn, actress

317
Katharine Hepburn

Among other things, Katharine Hepburn was famous for her delicious brownies. She often admonished visitors not to include too much flour in the mixture, and one taste of the results will demonstrate how right she was. She told *Time* magazine in 1980 that her figure was "the result of a lifetime of chocolate." So indulge, and perhaps you too will achieve a figure like Kate's.

318 *Katharine Hepburn's Brownies*

2 ounces unsweetened chocolate,
  roughly chopped
1/2 cup (1 stick) unsalted butter,
  plus more for the pan
1 cup sugar
2 large eggs, lightly beaten

1/2 teaspoon vanilla extract
1/4 cup all-purpose flour,
  plus more for the pan
1/4 teaspoon salt
1 cup coarsely chopped walnuts

Preheat the oven to 325°F. Butter and flour an 8-inch square baking pan and set aside.

Melt the chocolate with the butter in a small saucepan over very low heat, stirring occasionally until smooth. Set aside to cool. Stir in the sugar, then stir in the eggs and vanilla until smooth. Add the flour, salt, and nuts and stir until smooth. Pour the batter into the prepared pan. Bake about 40 minutes, or until a toothpick inserted in the center of the brownies comes out clean. Cool on a rack before cutting into bars.

Makes 16 brownies

Titans of Chocolate

319 Dr. James Baker
financed the first chocolate factory in the new world (the forerunner of Baker's Chocolate) in 1765 in Dorchester, Massachusetts Bay Colony.

320 Henri Nestlé
a Swiss chemist, developed a method of condensing milk while searching for a cure for a milk-borne disease that affected children.

321 Rudolph Lindt
at about the same time, developed the conching method which eliminated chocolate's grainy texture and gave it that beloved melt-in-your mouth quality.

322 Daniel Peter
Swiss confectioner and co-founder of the Nestlé company, blended condensed milk with chocolate liquor in 1876, after years of research, and gave the world milk chocolate.

323 Milton Snavely Hershey

a caramel maker from Lancaster, Pennsylvania, bought some new manufacturing machines he'd seen demonstrated at the Chicago World's Columbian Exposition in 1893 and began to mass-produce chocolate bars in the United States.

324 Frank Mars

and his wife, Ethel, started making and selling a variety of buttercream candies from the spotless kitchen of their home in Tacoma, Washington, in 1911. In 1920, after visiting a local drugstore with his son Forrest, Mars decided to produce a version of a chocolate malted that could be enjoyed anywhere. The result was the Milky Way bar, known in Europe as the Mars bar.

Chocolate Every Day

*Each day deserves a little chocolate and some days demand **a lot** of chocolate! And there's a chocolate that's just right for every day of the week.*

325 Monday

A Hershey's Hug or Kiss, tucked in your own or a family member's lunchbox.

326 Tuesday

A spoonful of hot fudge sauce straight from the fridge, followed by a spoonful of natural-style peanut butter—a breakfast of champions with an added protein boost.

327 Wednesday

A batch of extra-fudgy brownies to bring to the office. They'll help your fellow employees get through hump day.

328 Thursday

A Snickers bar from the vending machine—a midafternoon chocolate pick-me-up.

329 Friday

An after-work chocolate martini. TGIF!

330 Saturday

A banana split with chocolate ice cream, covered with chocolate syrup.

331 Sunday

A chocolate-chocolate cake from the bakery for Sunday dinner.

Chocolate For Breakfast

It's the most important meal of the day, so naturally breakfast should include a serious dose of chocolate.

332 Count Chocula

333 Cocoa Pebbles

334 Cocoa Krispies

335 Cocoa Puffs

336 Chocolate Pop-Tarts

337 Chocolate Waffles

338 Chocolate Chip Buttermilk Pancakes

339 Chocolate Chip Muffins

340 Pain au Chocolat

341 Chocolate-glazed chocolate doughnuts

342 Spiced Chocolate Chip Bundt Cake

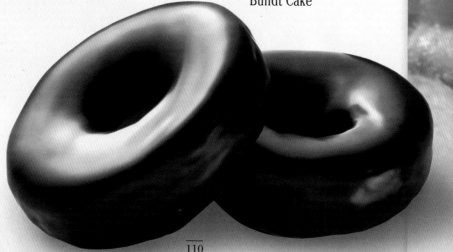

The Twelve Months of Chocolate

—◦◦◦—

Chocolate is one of the best ways to make for a sweet year.
Every single month is brightened by the addition of chocolate.
And, because of chocolate's versatility, it's easy to keep each
month interesting. Here are some ideas to start with:

344 February
Dark chocolate
bonbons from
a heart-shaped
red satin box

345 March
Chocolate sloops
from Harbor Sweets

346 April
A wedge of powdered
sugar-dusted flourless
chocolate cake

347 May
Streusel-topped
chocolate chunk
coffee cake

348 June
Long-stemmed dark
choclate roses

349 July
Hot fudge sauce over
2 scoops of vanilla ice
cream

350 August
A Good Humor
chocolate-covered
ice cream bar, bought
from the truck

351 September
Chocolate chip
cookies for after
school

352 October
A pocketful of mini-
chocolate bars for
tricks and treats

353 November
Hot chocolate to
keep your hands
warm at the football
game

354 December
An elegant chocolate
soufflé

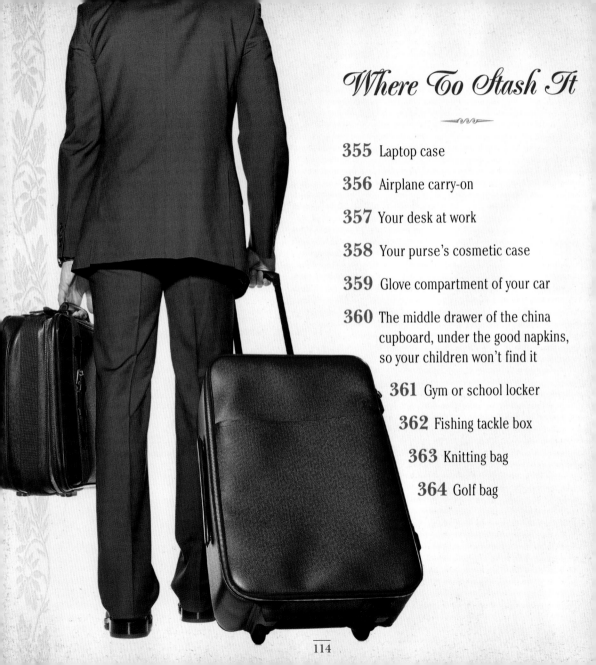

Where To Stash It

355 Laptop case

356 Airplane carry-on

357 Your desk at work

358 Your purse's cosmetic case

359 Glove compartment of your car

360 The middle drawer of the china cupboard, under the good napkins, so your children won't find it

361 Gym or school locker

362 Fishing tackle box

363 Knitting bag

364 Golf bag

Chocolate: Good for Morale

366 During the Civil War and World War II, the U.S. government recognized that in addition to providing nourishment, chocolate kept up the spirits of the troops.

367 Chocolate has made many flights into space, serving as comfort food for astronauts.

368 During World War II, 500,000 chocolate bars were produced every day for the U.S. Army.

Chocolate Entertainments

〰〰

*It's great to be an adult—You're old enough to have
an alcoholic beverage with your chocolate!*

369 Chocolate Cruises

Just like the Love Boat, chocolate cruises are where chocolate dreams come true.
Treasure hunts, chocolate tastings, and elaborate chocolate buffets, along with onboard
experts, lectures, and trips to the cradles of chocolate in Central and South America.

370 Chocolate Festivals

They come in all sizes, from a local or national charity to a big bash put on by a mega
hotel. They offer competitions, prizes ("Win Your Weight in Chocolate!"), artwork, and
demonstrations. One thing holds true for all of them—there are plenty of chocolate
samples to be enjoyed.

371 Chocolate Sommeliers

The Ritz Carlton in Philadelphia employs a hot-chocolate sommelier. The staff member's
duties consist of heating milk and half-and-half and suggesting a flavored whipped
cream to accompany guests' cocoa. The hot chocolate program offers marshmallows
created by the pastry kitchen in flavors such as chocolate, berry, and lavender/citrus.

372 Chocolate Room Service

The Hotel Meurice in Paris has a Chocolate Breakfast. The special breakfast tray is
laden with chocolate brioches and pains au chocolat (croissants filled with chocolate),
chocolate-flavored breakfast cereals, warm chocolate cake, and handmade chocolate
cookies and brownies. It is served with tea, coffee, and, of course, hot chocolate.
There's even a chocolate-scented pen to sign the bill.

373 Chocolate Nightclubs

Sugar is a Chicago club that pairs decadent desserts with dessert wines, martinis, and champagne. One sixty**blue**, also in Chicago, introduced a cocoa bar menu in its lounge.

A Chocolate Buzz

374
Chocolate martini

375
Chocolate vodka

376
Kahlua

377
Young's Double Chocolate Stout

378
Brooklyn Black Chocolate Stout

379
Zucca—a port wine with
chocolate flavor and aroma

380
Vermeer—Maurice Kanbar,
founder of Skyy vodka, created
this chocolate cream liqueur,
which is made from Dutch
chocolate, fresh dairy cream
from the Netherlands,
and premium vodka.

381
Godiva Liqueur, Godiva White
Chocolate Liqueur, Godiva
Cappuccino Liqueur

382 The Chocotini

A most delicious chocolate martini, from the discriminating author of *Drinkology,* James Waller.

White crème de cacao and unsweetened cocoa powder,
    for rimming the glass
2 ounces vodka
1 ounce white crème de cacao
Chocolate chips

Rim a chilled cocktail glass with the crème de cacao and cocoa powder. (To do this, pour a small amount of crème de cacao onto a saucer or small plate, swishing it around until it covers the plate's surface. Spoon some cocoa powder onto a separate plate, and spread it around as evenly as you can. Now, upend the cocktail glass onto the crème de cacao-covered plate, immediately transferring it to the cocoa–covered plate. Twist the glass until the entire rim is coated.) Combine the vodka and crème de cacao in a mixing glass, with ice. Stir, and strain into the prepared cocktail glass. Garnish with a few chocolate chips.

Makes 1 drink

Chocolate On Display

A Box of Chocolates

394
The satin ribbon

395
The aroma as you lift the lid

396
The quilted paper that protects them

397
The pleated paper cups that hold each one

398
The diagram on the inside of the lid identifying each kind

399
The way the nuts stick out of the enrobed pieces

400
Sharing with someone who likes the pieces you dislike

401
Not having to share with *anyone*

402
The squiggles on top

The Inside Story

Whether it is a chocolate bar or a box of chocolates, most of us have decided preferences as to what we want when we bite into a chocolate. Here are some of the many possibilities.

403 Nougat

404 Marshmallow fluff

405 Caramel

406 Ganache

407 Fruit cordial

408 Dried fruit

409 Nuts

410 Crisped rice

411 Orange cream

412 Raspberry cream

413 Chocolate mousse

414 Coconut

415 Toffee bits

416 Fruit pectin

oro che vivono d'amore vivono d'eterni

lives on love lives on forever.

The Medium is the Message

As if a simple gift of chocolate were not eloquent enough, some chocolates say it with words.

417
Chocowits
Chocolates with message cards

418
Dove Promises
Each chocolate contains an inspirational message

419
Baci chocolates
Each Baci includes a poetic love note written in 4 languages

420
Chocolate fortune cookies
Wisdom with flavor

Perfect Pairings

Meltingly Delicious

Restaurant customers are increasingly requesting and ordering warm chocolate desserts that "melt," and chefs are happy to oblige.

440
Chocolate fondue with sliced rounds of warm, caramelized, banana-filled crepes for dipping

441
Chocolate-cardamom pots de crème served with warm milk chocolate

442
White chocolate "raviolis" made by filling sweet pastry dough with frozen balls of ganache and then deep-frying to order

443
Chocolate soufflé with its crusty top and warm, soft and gooey interior, served with a cold scoop of vanilla bean ice cream

444
Molten chocolate cake with frozen ganache added to the center before baking for extra ooze

445 Baker's® Molten Chocolate Cake

Most people find a warm, meltingly gooey center in a chocolate dessert irresistible. These molten cakes capture that quite deliciously.

6 squares (1 package) Baker's Bittersweet Baking Chocolate
10 tablespoons (1 1/4 sticks) unsalted butter
1 1/2 cups powdered sugar, plus more for serving
1/2 cup all-purpose flour
3 whole eggs
3 egg yolks
Fresh raspberries for garnish (optional)

Preheat the oven to 425°F. Grease six (6-ounce) custard cups or soufflé dishes and place them on a baking sheet.

Place the chocolate and butter in a large microwavable bowl and microwave on High 2 minutes, or until the butter is melted. Stir the mixture until the chocolate is completely melted. Add the powdered sugar and flour; and mix well. Add the whole eggs and egg yolks and whisk together until well blended. Divide the batter evenly among the prepared custard cups.

Bake for 14 to 15 minutes or until the cakes are firm around edges but still soft in the centers. Let stand 1 minute. Run a small knife around the cakes to loosen them. Carefully invert the cakes onto dessert dishes. Sprinkle with additional powdered sugar and garnish with fresh raspberries, if desired. Serve immediately.

Make-ahead tip: Batter can be made the day ahead and poured into prepared custard cups. Cover the filled cups with plastic wrap and refrigerate. When you're ready to bake, uncover the batter and proceed with the recipe.

Makes 6 servings

446
German Chocolate Cake

The "German" in German Chocolate Cake comes not from the country, but from the sweet chocolate baking bar, similar to milk chocolate, that was developed for Baker's Chocolate Company in 1852 by Sam German. The original name of the recipe was German's Chocolate Cake, but over the years the apostrophe and the "s" have dropped off, leading many to assume that the cake is German. German Chocolate Cake gained widespread popularity in 1957, thanks to a Dallas housewife who sent the recipe to a local newspaper. The spike in sales of German's Sweet Chocolate alerted the manufacturer, and copies of the recipe quickly started popping up in newspapers across the nation. In one year, sales jumped 73%. Today there are a variety of mixes available for the sweet chocolate cake with coconut-pecan topping, as well as a variety of spin-off products, including German chocolate pies, brownies, and cheesecakes. So, in spite of its name, German Chocolate Cake is as American as, well, you know.

*No matter where you are,
chocolate is always chocolate.*

—Sana Blom

447

It melts in your hand, so you have some left for later.

448

It also melts in your pockets, under your nails, and it sometimes
gets stuck between your teeth—all great for snacking.

449

Chocolate fills up your stomach, leaving no room for fattening
things like spinach, liver, and turnips.

450

It can be eaten at every meal and you never get tired of it.

451

It can be dressed up in a soufflé or dressed down
in chocolate chip cookies.

452

It can go anywhere and is always appropriate.

453

It feels good going down.

454

You can shave it, curl it, and mold it,
yet it has nothing to do with hair.

455 The first known recipe for brownies appeared in the Sears, Roebuck Catalogue in 1897.

Brownies

456

Brownies are classified as a bar cookie, and are a cross between a cake and a cookie.

457

No one knows the exact origin of brownies. One popular story credits Mildred Schrumpf, a home economics teacher from Maine, for accidentally creating these dense, fudgy squares when she forgot to add baking powder to a cake she was demonstrating to her class.

458

There are two schools of thought when it comes to baking brownies: One aims for a dense and fudgy texture; the other prefers a more cake-like concoction.

459

All brownies contain the same basic ingredients (chocolate, butter, eggs, sugar, and flour), though every baker has his or her own opinion on the *type* of chocolate that works best.

460

Brownie add-ins include nuts (walnuts, pecans, hazelnuts, or macadamia), fruit (apricot), and other flavors (ganache, expresso powder, peanut butter, mint).

461

The two kinds of people: Those who love nuts in their brownies, and those who loathe nuts in their brownies.

Great Chocolate Cookbook Authors

Death by Chocolate
The Last Word On A Consuming Passion

FRANÇOIS PAYARD
from New York's Famous Pâtisserie and Bistro

140 Classic Desserts *for the* Home Baker

SIMPLY *Sensational* DESSERTS

THE ART OF
chocolate

techniques & recipes for simply spectacular desserts & confections

ELAINE GONZÁLEZ

photographs by Frankie Frankeny

CHOCOLATE DESSERTS BY
Pierre Hermé

WRITTEN BY
Dorie Greenspan
Author of *Baking with Julia*

Like Water for Chocolate

A Novel in Monthly Installments with Recipes, Romances, and Home Remedies

"A mystical Mexican love story that will charm the [p...] and the heart..."
—USA Today

R O A L D   D A H L

ILLUSTRATED BY QUENTIN BLAKE

Charlie
and the
Chocolate
Factory

A DELICIOUSLY DEVILISH NOVEL BY THE NEW YORK TIMES
BESTSELLING AUTHOR OF STICKS & SCONES

DIANE MOTT
DAVIDSON

DYNAMITE

BANTAM BOOKS

DYING FOR
CHOCOLATE

474
*Charlie and the
Chocolate Factory*
By Roald Dahl

Great Chocolate Books

Diet Chocolate

*Who says you have to give up chocolate
to lose weight?*

481 Chocolate-covered raisins

482 Chocolate-covered peanuts

483 Chocolate chip granola bars

484 Chocolate-dipped fruit such as
strawberries and dried apricots

485 Chocolate Slim-Fast shakes

486 Dark chocolate bark

487 Krave Bars

488 Lowfat chocolate milk

489 Lowfat chocolate pudding

490 Sweet Escapes

Ways To Eat Chocolate

491 Oreo cookies
Eat the middle first and save the outside for last.

492 Peanut M&M's
Bite the middle and get the peanut out.

493 Butterfinger Bars
Eat the chocolate edges first and then the center.

494 Reese's Peanut Butter Cups
Eat around the peanut butter filling and then nibble the last of the chocolate off.

495 Boxed chocolates
Stick a finger in the bottom of the chocolate to find out what flavor it is.

496 Cadbury Eggs
Poke a hole in the middle and suck out all of the caramel.

497 Brownies
Sandwich softened ice cream between a couple.

498 Chocolate-covered cherries
Bite off the top and lick out the center of the candy.

499 Buster Bars
Eat off the chocolate shell.

500 M&M's
Suck off the candy coating.

501 Chocolate cake
Devour the chocolate frosting first, then tackle the cake.

Kisses and Hugs

Beloved since their introduction on July 1, 1907, Hershey's® Kisses® brand chocolates have been a diminuitive sweet treat beloved by all, whether you eat them one at a time or devour an entire bag. By the way, there are 95 Kisses® in a pound.

502 The kissing sound made by the machines as they turn out millions of Kisses®. Hershey can make over 33 million Kisses every day at its factories in Hershey, PA and in California.

503 The signature blue-and-white label

504 Kisses with almonds

505 Hugs® with almonds

506 All the other seasonal wrapper colors (Hershey started making Kisses with red, green, and silver foil for Christmas in 1962.)

507 Collecting all the used foil wrappers into a big ball as you eat the Kisses

508 Filling champagne glasses with Kisses as wedding favors

509 Giving special Kisses for special occasions

510 A single Hershey's Kisses® chocolate is only a half-point in the Weight Watchers plan.

511 The Hershey's Kissmobile® Cruiser is 25 feet long, 11 feet high, 8 feet wide, and it has 3 flags.

512 **The silver foil wrapper**

513
Black-and-white cookies

514
Nonpareils

515
**Chocolate-coated vanilla
ice cream**

Girl Scout Cookies

*Just like soup and sandwich, Girl Scouts and cookies go hand in hand.
A major revenue source for the Girl Scouts, selling cookies becomes many girls'
first exposure to big business. Chocolate cookies outsell the rest.*

16 Thin Mints
The #1, best-selling Girl Scout cookie: thin cookie wafers dipped in a chocolate coating and flavored with pure peppermint oil.

17 Tagalongs
Crisp vanilla cookies covered with a real peanut-butter filling and then drenched in a luscious chocolate coating.

18 Samoas
Vanilla cookies covered with caramel on top and bottom, then rolled in toasted coconut and striped with a rich chocolate coating.

19 Double Dutch
Rich chocolate cookie dough mixed with milk chocolate chips.

520 All Abouts
These shortbread cookies are made with a Girl Scout message embossed on top and coated with rich chocolate fudge on the bottom.

521 Edy's Girl Scout Cookie ice cream
Introduced in 2004 in three limited-edition favorite flavors: Samoas, Tagalongs, and Thin Mints.

522 S'Mores
Invented by Girl Scouts, these melted concoctions (milk chocolate bars and marshmallows sandwiched between graham crackers) taste best cooked over a well-stoked campfire.

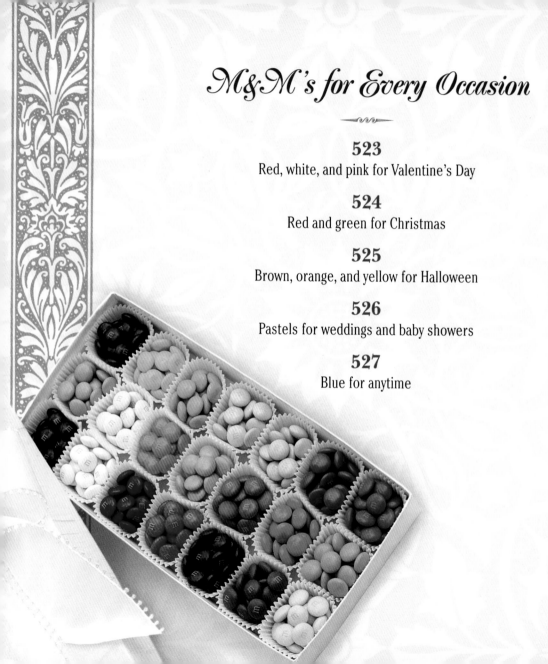

M&M's for Every Occasion

523
Red, white, and pink for Valentine's Day

524
Red and green for Christmas

525
Brown, orange, and yellow for Halloween

526
Pastels for weddings and baby showers

527
Blue for anytime

Under Wraps

528 The yellow and brown bag of Nestlé chocolate chips

529 The blueness of the Almond Joy wrapper

530 The redness of the Mounds wrapper

531 The brown wrappers of Hershey's bars

532 The silver wrappers of York Peppermint Patties

533 The chunky shape of a Chunky

534 The triangular shape of Toblerone bars

Hot Chocolate

535
With marshmallows

536
With whipped cream

537
With chocolate shavings

538
With a candy-cane stirrer

539
With peppermint schnapps

540
With coffee

541
Frozen hot chocolate
from Serendipity

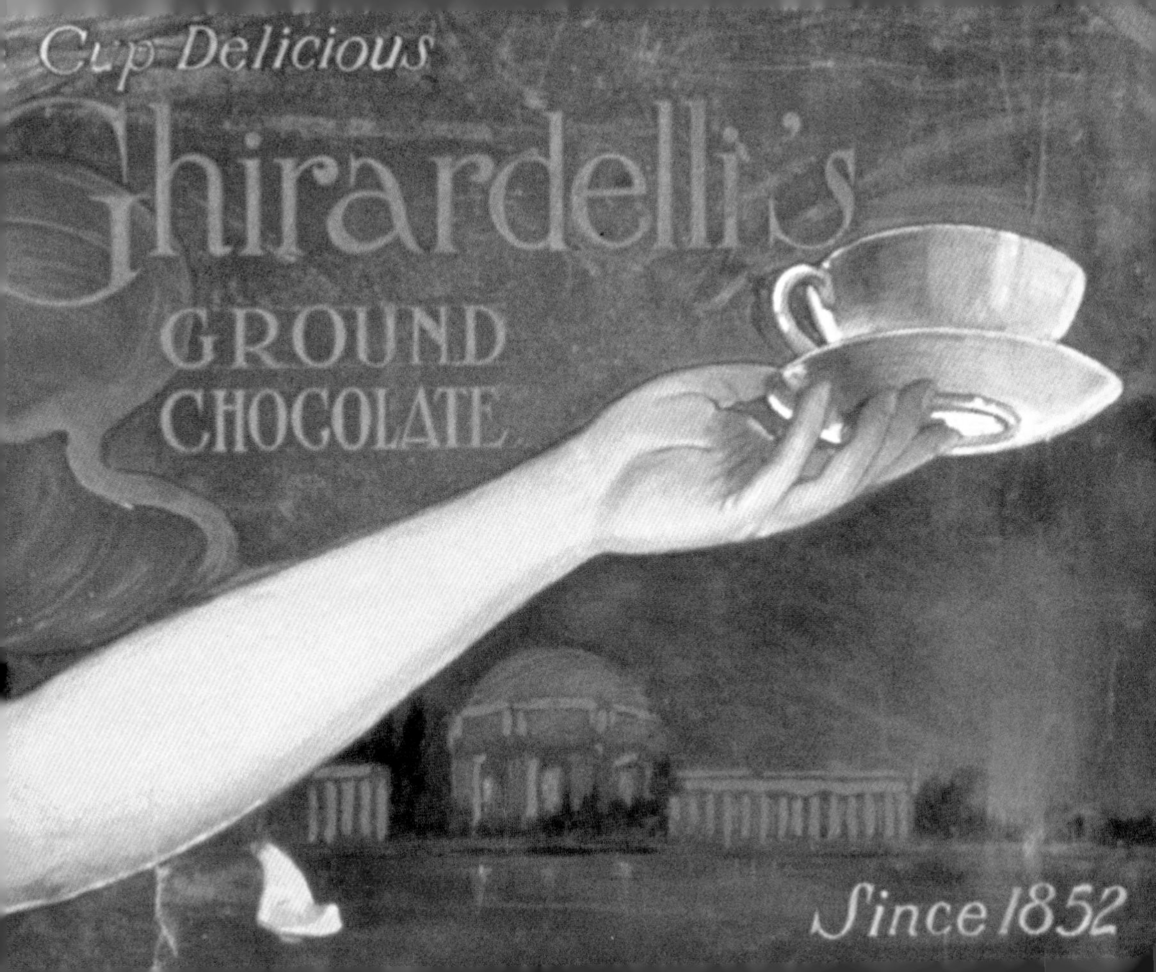
Cup Delicious
Ghirardelli's
GROUND
CHOCOLATE
Since 1852

542
Thick, Rich Hot Chocolate

This very chocolatey, grownup version of hot chocolate warms you up inside and out.

2 ounces high-quality bittersweet chocolate, coarsely chopped
3/4 cup milk
1/8 teaspoon vanilla extract

Place the chocolate in a 1-cup microwave-safe measuring cup. Microwave on High for 1 to 2 minutes, or until the chocolate is melted. (The chocolate may appear to hold its shape even if it is melted.)

Gradually whisk in the milk until combined. Rerun the cup to the microwave oven and heat for 30 to 60 seconds longer, or until the mixture is heated through. Stir in the vanilla.

Makes 1 decadent serving

543 Chile-chocolate truffles

Sweet and Hot

544
At the Cerén archaeological site in El Salvador, researchers discovered painted ceramic storage vessels that contained large quantities of chile seed with cacao.

545
What was probably the first recipe for a chocolate drink was published in Spain in 1644 by Antonio Colmenero de Ledesma in his book, *A Curious Treatise of the Nature and Quality of Chocolate*. The recipe contained chiles, anise, cinnamon, vanilla, hazelnuts, sugar, and annatto seeds.

546
A chocolate habanero chile variety rates highest on the heat scale of all chiles tested in 2001 at New Mexico State University.

547
Spicy chocolate popcorn

548
Habanero chocolate bars

Sweet and Cold

549 Clown Sundaes—Vanilla ice cream with marshmallow sauce, chocolate sauce, and Spanish peanuts

550 Chocolate ice cream

551 Chocolate chip ice cream

552 Chocolate chip cookie dough ice cream

553 Rocky Road ice cream

554 Tin Roof Sundaes—Vanilla ice cream topped with hot fudge sauce and Spanish peanuts

555 Chocolate-covered frozen banana

556 Marshmallow fudge ice cream

557 Fudge pecan ice cream

558 Chocolate frozen yogurt

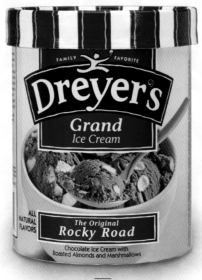

560 Danish

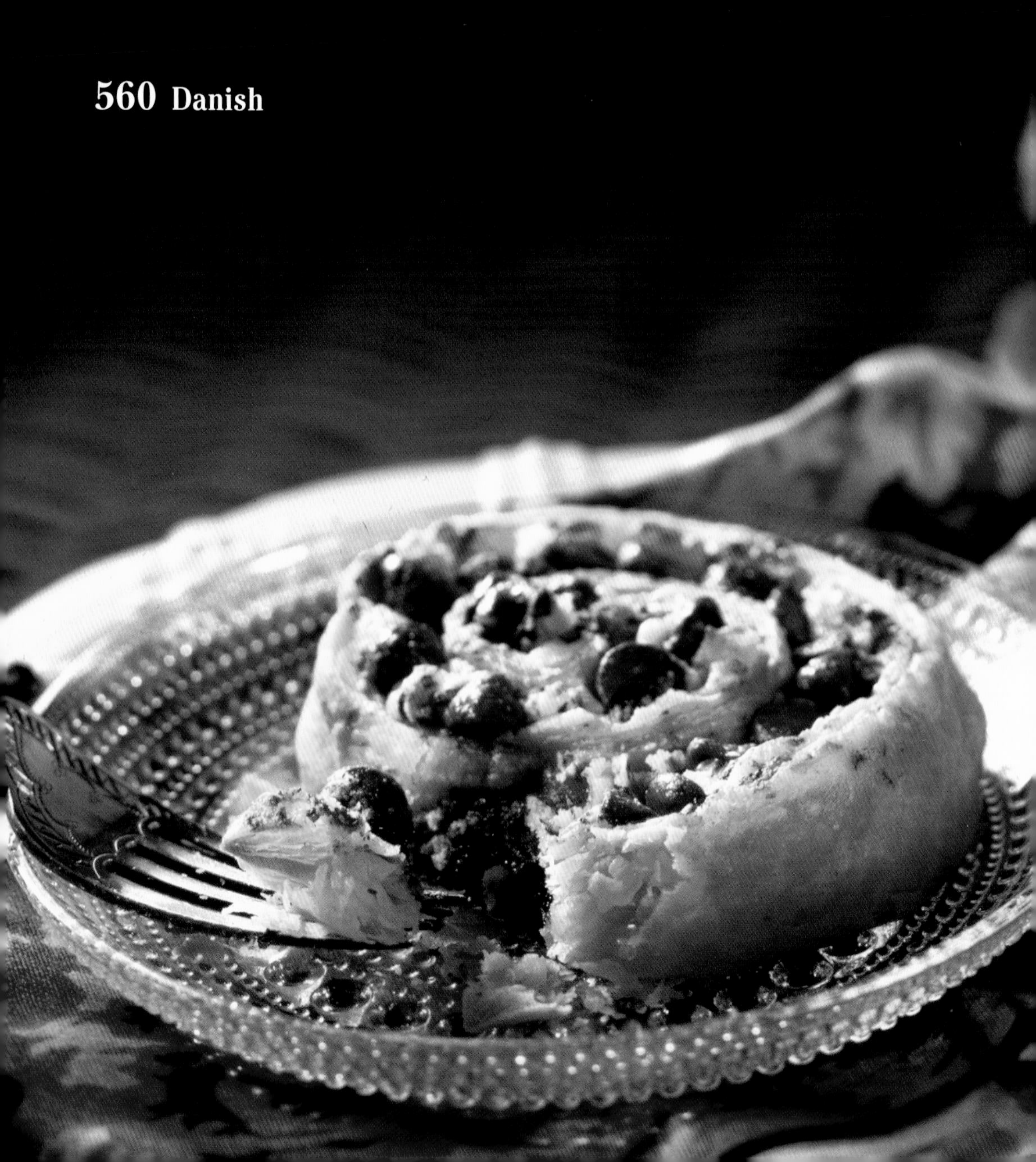

Just Add Chocolate

These foods and dishes are all wonderful. They're even more wonderful when chocolate is added.

561 Bagels	**572** Malt
562 Cheesecake	**573** Meringue
563 Chili	**574** Mole
564 Cream pie	**575** Mousse
565 Crêpes	**576** Pies
566 Croissants	**577** Puddings
567 Crunch	**578** Shakes
568 Doughnuts	**579** Soufflés
569 Éclairs	**580** Stews
570 Flan	**581** Sundaes
571 Graham crackers	**582** Trifle

Chocolate Sauces and Syrups

Sweet chocolate syrup or rich chocolate sauce, whichever you prefer, makes a decadent addition to ice cream, desserts, and drinks. Chocolate syrup was even used as a stand-in for blood in the famous shower scene in Alfred Hitchcock's movie, "Psycho!"

583 Bittersweet Chocolate Sauce

584 Bittersweet Chocolate Sour Cream Sauce

585 Bittersweet Chocolate Syrup

586 Black Chocolate Sauce

587 Chocolate Fondue Sauce

588 Chocolate Syrup

589 Chocolate Walnut Sauce

590 Cinnamon Chocolate Sauce

591 Deep Dark Chocolate Sauce

592 Hot Fudge Sauce

593 Chocolate Almond Sauce

594 Chocolate Peppermint Sauce

595 Hot Peanut Fudge Sauce

596 Milk Chocolate Mallow Fudge Sauce

597 Mint Fudge Sauce

598
Made-from-Scratch, All-Purpose Old-Fashioned Chocolate Syrup

This easy recipe for chocolate syrup is good for all sorts of uses —for the Chocolate Egg Cream (recipe on page 78), to flavor milk shakes, pour over ice cream, or simply in a drippy spoonful "as is."

1/2 cup light corn syrup
1/4 cup water
1/3 cup unsweetened cocoa powder
1/3 cup sugar
1 teaspoon vanilla extract

Combine the corn syrup, water, cocoa powder, and sugar in a small heavy saucepan. Cook the mixture over high heat, stirring constantly, until it comes to a boil. Continue stirring constantly, for 1 minute.

Remove the pan from the heat and stir in the vanilla. Cool and store the syrup in an airtight container; it can be kept in the refrigerator for up to 10 days.

Makes about 3/4 cup of syrup

CACAO VAN HOUTEN

MEILLEUR QUE TOUS LES CHOCOLATS.
T.S.V.P.

Fudge

*Creamy, semi-soft, and unabashedly sweet,
fudge is a decadent mixture of sugar, butter, cream,
corn syrup, and various flavorings.*

599

Chocolate is the most popular type of fudge, though fudge
can also be flavored with maple, butterscotch,
vanilla, peanut butter, and more.

600

Fudge either can be smooth or contain nuts,
chocolate chips, or candied fruit.

601

This decadent treat was invented over 100 years ago in the
United States, though the exact origin is widely disputed.

602

Fudge is believed to be the result of a culinary accident
involving a bungled batch of caramels.

603

Penuche is made with brown sugar, cream, and butter
and is firmer than traditional fudge. The name comes
from the Mexican word for "raw sugar."

It's All Academic

—∞—

*The earliest documentation of fudge appears in a letter written
in 1886 by Emily Battersby Hartridge, a Vassar College student.
Ms. Hartridge refers to a fudge recipe that was given to her by a classmate's
cousin. She used it to make 30 pounds of fudge to sell at a senior auction.
Word spread, and the other women's colleges soon followed
with their own versions.*

604
Vassar College Fudge
White sugar, cream, unsweetened chocolate, butter

605
Wellesley College Fudge
White sugar, heavy cream, unsweetened chocolate, butter, marshmallows

606
Smith College Fudge
Butter, white sugar, brown sugar, heavy cream, molasses,
unsweetened chocolate, vanilla

607
Herbert's Candies

The country's first roadside candy store, accessible to travelers on Interstate 84 between Connecticut and New York. Herbert's produces approximately 3,000 pounds of fudge a week.

608
Chocolate Black Walnut Fudge

609
Chocolate Cashew Fudge

610
Chocolate Rum Fudge

611
Chocolate Chip Fudge

612
Chocolate Mint Fudge

613
Chocolate Peanut Butter Fudge

614
Chocolate Cherry Cordial Fudge

615
Chocolate Chocolate Fudge

616
Rocky Road Fudge

617
Triple Chip Fudge

618 Mamie Eisenhower's Million Dollar Fudge

Former first lady Mamie Eisenhower was known for her Million Dollar Fudge. This recipe yields a generous amount of rich, delicious candy, perfect for holiday gift-giving.

1/2 cup (1 stick) butter or margarine
4 1/2 cups of sugar
One 13-ounce can evaporated milk
Three 8-ounce packages semisweet chocolate, broken in half
One 7-ounce jar marshmallow cream
3 cups chopped pecans
1 teaspoon salt
1 teaspoon vanilla

Combine the butter, sugar, and milk in a heavy 4-quart saucepan and bring to a full rolling boil, stirring constantly. Boil for 5 minutes over medium heat, stirring constantly to prevent scorching.

Remove the pan from the heat. Gradually stir in the chocolate pieces until melted. Add the marshmallow cream, pecans, salt, and vanilla and stir until well blended.

Grease a 15 by 10-inch pan and set aside.

Spread the fudge evenly on the prepared pan and chill, uncovered, until firm, about 30 minutes. Cut into 60 squares, using a sharp paring knife.

Nutella

*This chocolate hazelnut spread was created in Italy in the 1940s
by Pietro Ferrero, a pastry maker and founder of the Fererro Company.
Due to war rationing, there was a shortage of chocolate, so Ferrero mixed cocoa
with toasted hazelnuts to create a more affordable spread. It was first called
"Pasta Gianduja." In 1964 it was renamed Nutella®. Worldwide,
it outsells all peanut butter brands combined.*

619 Nutella in a crêpe with peach preserves and chocolate sauce drizzled on top

620 Nutella spread on apple slices

621 Popcorn dipped in Nutella

622 Nutella spread on matzoh

623 Nutella–peanut butter sandwich

624 Nutella slathered on a banana

Chocolate Destinations

25 Ghirardelli Square

The California gold rush brought Domingo Ghirardelli and his chocolate to San Francisco. His chocolate business grew so much that in 1893 Domingo and his sons purchased an entire block of city property. While the chocolate is not manufactured there today, the sign still remains and Ghirardelli Square was granted a National Historic Register status. The square offers shopping, entertainment, and waterfront dining near Fisherman's Wharf.

26 La Cabosse d'Or Miniature Golf Theme Park

This gigantic miniature golf park in Quebec City, Quebec, is all about chocolate. Each hole has a different chocolate theme as well as plaques giving information about chocolate in both French and English.

27 Chocolate Bar

This is a modern emporium in New York City where a dozen or so truffles washed down with hot chocolate make the perfect meal.

628 Chocolate Cascade

The only chocolate fountain in the U.S. is located in the lobby of the Candy Basket Chocolate Factory in Portland, Oregon. More than 2,000 pounds of melted chocolate fall and flow 20 feet over a sculpted marble-and-bronze fountain.

629 Hershey Town, USA

Billed as "The Sweetest Place on Earth," this is a world-class theme park with rides and attractions devoted to chocolate.

Miniature Railway and Lake, Hershey Park

630 Chain store chocolates

In the early part of the twentieth century, a young man would seldom go to pick up a date without bringing her a bouquet of flowers or a box of chocolates. (For formal affairs, he would bring or send a corsage to pin on her formal gown.) The box of chocolates would usually be purchased at an independent drug store, of which there were between 50,000 and 75,000 in 1940. Whitman's of Philadelphia and Schrafft's of Boston were the larger chocolate companies in this category, but there were hundreds of others.

There were also some regional candy chain stores, but nothing national: no one had yet breached the Rockies. The largest chain in the country was Fanny Farmer, at that time limited to New England and the Middle Atlantic States. They had two factories servicing about 100 to 200 little candy stores. There was Loft, limited to Metropolitan New York, New Jersey, and the Philadelphia area. In Chicago, there were Mrs. Stevens Candies and Mrs. Snyder's Candies. In Denver, Kansas City, and Lincoln, Nebraska, there was Mrs. Stover's Bungalow Candies. The name was later changed to Russell Stover Candies. (But Clara Stover had her revenge—she outlived Russell by many years.)

—Samuel R. Kostick, former Vice President, Loft Candy Company

American Chocolate

The saying "as American as apple pie" notwithstanding,
the United States is a nation of chocolate lovers.

631 A study by the Gallup Organization found chocolate to be America's favorite flavor. Its popularity surpassed that of other leading flavors, including vanilla, by a 3 to 1 ratio. Chocolate even outranked those old-fashioned favorites strawberry, cherry, banana, butterscotch, and coffee.

632 Americans like milk chocolate; Europeans tend to prefer dark chocolate.

633 American candy bars are often made by wrapping chocolate around a filling. Europeans prefer solid bars studded with dried fruits and nuts.

634 In the U.S., 8 out of 10 households use chocolate, whether in desserts, snacks, or beverages.

All-American Classics:
Chocolate Bars

—◦∿◦—

635
Snickers, the most popular candy bar in the United States of America

636 Dove Chocolate Bar

637 Hershey's Bar

638 Mr. Goodbar

639 Mounds

640 Almond Joy

641 Milky Way

642 Kit Kat

643 5th Avenue

644 Chunky

645 Heath Bar

646 Twix

647 Baby Ruth

648 Kudos

649 100 Grand

650 Butterfinger Bars

651 Crunch

652 Oh Henry!

All-American Classics:
Small Pleasures

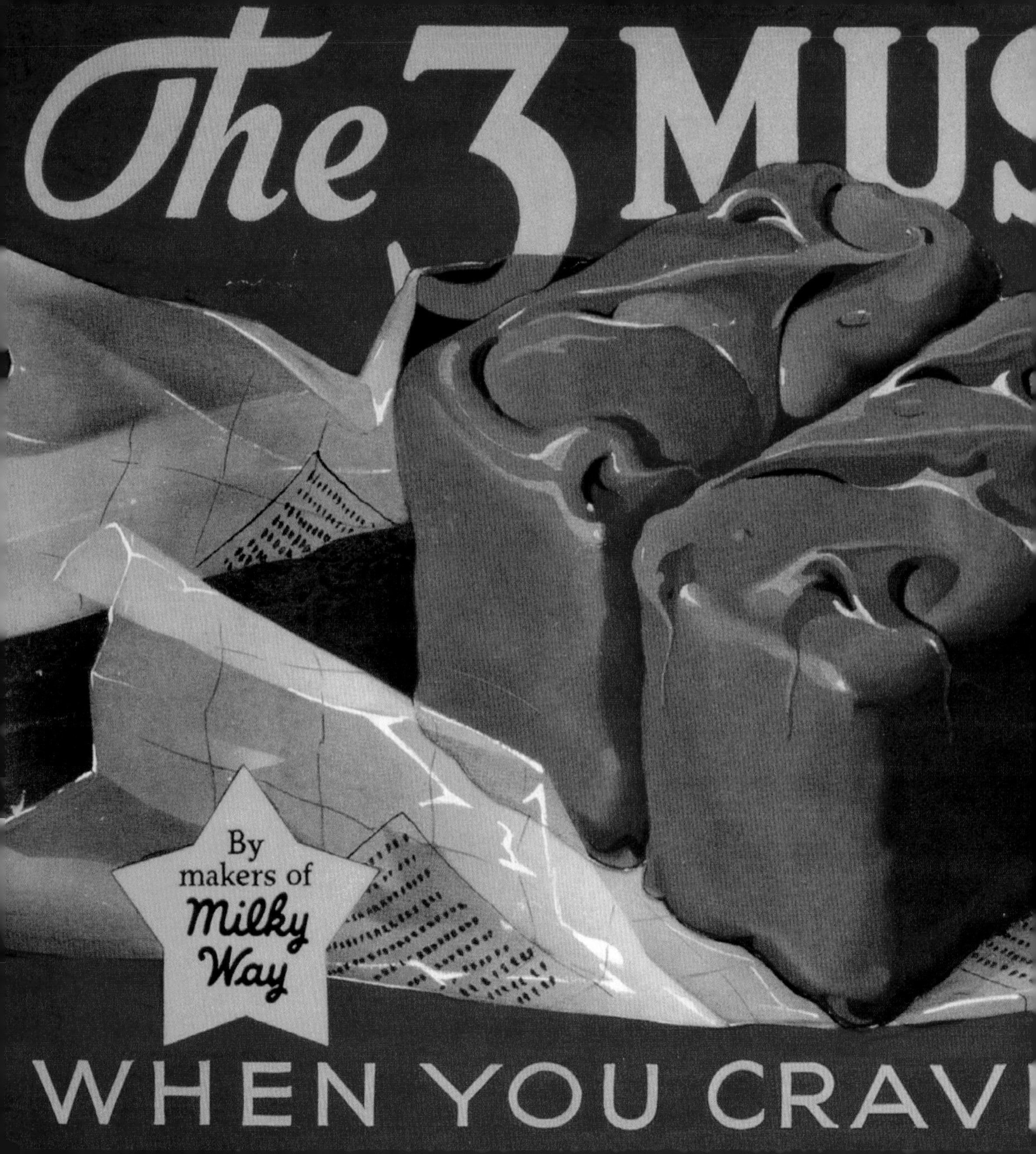
The 3 MUS
By makers of Milky Way
WHEN YOU CRAV

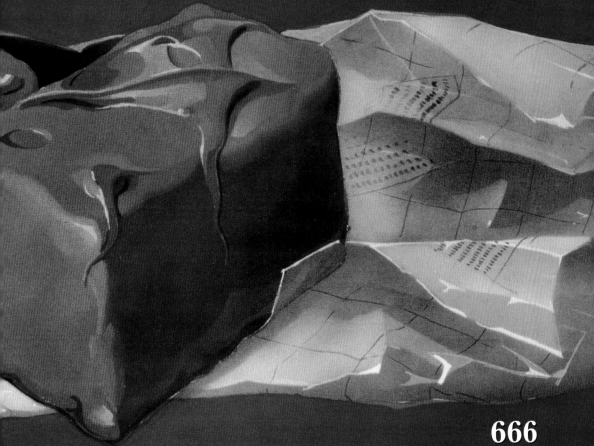

KETEERS

GOOD CANDY

666
Three
Musketeers

667
All-American Chocolate Pudding

A combination of unsweetened chocolate and bittersweet chocolate give this pudding its rich chocolate flavor.

1 cup sugar
1/3 cup cornstarch
Pinch of salt
3 large egg yolks, lightly beaten
4 cups whole milk
6 ounces bittersweet chocolate, finely chopped
2 ounces unsweetened chocolate, finely chopped
2 teaspoons vanilla extract

Stir together the sugar, cornstarch, and salt in a heavy large saucepan. Gradually whisk in the egg yolks until combined, then gradually whisk in the milk.

Cook the mixture over medium heat, stirring constantly with the whisk, for about 10 minutes, or until the mixture thickens and comes to a boil. Remove the pan from the heat and whisk in the bittersweet and unsweetened chocolate and vanilla until smooth. Quickly pour the mixture through a strainer into a large bowl. Cover the surface of the pudding with a piece of plastic wrap to prevent a skin from forming. Refrigerate until chilled.

Makes 6 large servings

HOMETOWN DELICIOUS

668
Malley's Chocolates

—✦—

*Founded in 1935 during the Great Depression,
Mike Malley started with a simple copper pot set over
an open flame. This Cleveland, Ohio, family business
has grown to 14 stores, many of them also including
ice cream parlors. A signature chocolate is
the Pecan Billybob—crunchy roasted pecans
covered with caramel and coated
with milk chocolate.*

669
Mitchell's

—✦—

*Light, chocolate-coated marshmallow
squares, which would be sold on Saturday
nights to nearby moviegoers, are a beloved favorite
from this Cleveland shop, founded in 1939
by Greek immigrant Chris Mitchell.*

Regional Chocolate

670 Goo Goo Cluster

Based in Nashville, Tennessee. Founder Howell Campbell was one of the first to develop a candy bar that included multiple ingredients. Goo Goo Clusters combine peanuts, caramel, marshmallow, and milk chocolate in a round cluster. The original 1912 advertisement for this bar proclaimed it to be a "nourishing lunch for a nickel."

671 Idaho Spud Bar

Based in Boise, Idaho, the Idaho Candy Company is most famous for these potato-shaped bars, which were invented in 1918. A light cocoa-flavored marshmallow center is drenched with a dark chocolate coating and then sprinkled with coconut.

672 Twin Bing

The Palmer Candy Company of Sioux City, Iowa, introduced this candy bar in the 1920s. The original Bing has a cherry cream center covered with a chocolatey-peanut coating. The Crispy Peanut Butter Caramel Twin Bing has a creamy peanut butter/caramel center surrounded by a crispy chocolaty coating.

673 Chocolate Cherry Mash

Launched in St. Joseph, Missouri, by the Chase Candy Company around 1918. First known as Cherry Chase and then Cherry Chaser, Cherry Mash is a quarter-pound mound of chopped, roasted peanuts blended with a chocolate coating over a smooth cherry fondant center.

674 Mallo Cup

Made by Boyer Brothers of Altoona, Pennsylvania, a company that specializes in manufacturing cup candies. Mallo Cup is made with a milk chocolate coating with coconut and a whipped marshmallow cream center.

675 Marshall Field's Frango® Mint Chocolates

The legendary Chicago department store brought this Seattle confection, originally named Franco, to Chicago in 1929. (The name was changed to Frango during the Spanish Civil War.) The still-secret recipe combines 3 kinds of chocolate, with more chocolate and less mint flavoring than typical mint chocolate. A little added salt enhances the flavor.

676 Valomilk

A gooey, marshmallow-filled chocolate cup made in Merriam, Kansas by Russell Sifers.

Whitman's Sampler

Whitman's Candies was founded in 1842.
The Sampler, introduced in 1912, is the best-selling box
of chocolate in the country. A Sampler is sold every 1.5 seconds!
What's inside those familiar boxes? The map is printed
on the inside cover.

677 Butter Cream Caramel

678 Chocolate Truffle

679 Chocolate Covered
Almonds

680 Chocolate Covered
Peanuts

681 Chocolate Nut Fudge

682 Vermont Fudge

683 Cherry Cordial

684 Chocolate Whip

685 Molasses Chew

686 Almond Nougat

687 Pecan/Walnut Cluster

688 Cashew Cluster

689 Vanilla Butter Cream

690 Toffee Chips

691 Chocolate Covered
Coconut

692 Solid Chocolate
Messenger Boy

Fran's Chocolates

Founder Fran Bigelow launched her business in 1982 from a quaint
Seattle storefront. Bigelow prepares the chocolates in small batches and uses
no preservatives or artificial additives. While many of her chocolates are based on
traditional European methods, she continues to create new products, including cakes,
bars, sauces, baking products, and ice cream. Among Fran's creations:

693
Milk Smoked Salt Caramels

Soft, fresh caramels dipped in a 42% rich blend of dark & milk chocolates
and sprinkled with smoked sea salt harvested off the coast of Wales.

694
Spiced Macadamia

Slow-roasted macadamia nuts coated in caramelized sugar, hand-rolled
in Spanish hot-smoked paprika and chili powder with a dash of kosher salt,
then dipped in dark chocolate and dusted with cocoa powder.

695
Chocolaterie Bernard Callebaut

—◦◦◦—

Started in Canada in 1982 by Bernard Callebaut,
a descendent of the owners of the Callebaut Chocolate factory in
Wieze, Belgium. Callebaut's family owned the company from 1911
until 1980, when it was sold to the Suchard Toblerone group. The Callebaut
family produced large quantities of world-class chocolate, but Bernard was
the first of his family to begin producing small chocolates, called pralines
in Belgium. Bernard is well known for his attention to sourcing out
the ingredients used for filling the pralines, and he uses
approximately 47 different centers with an additional
20 seasonally-offered centers.

696
Chocolate Moderne

—⚮—

Former banker Joan Coukos left the money scene behind
after discovering world-class chocolates on the Place du Grand Sablon in Brussels.
Honing her chocolate-making skills, Coukos opened Chocolate Moderne in New York City
in 2003. Her chocolates include the Snake Charmer, The Player, Caramel Caresse,
Raspberry Rendez-vous, La Dolce Grapefruit, Hazelnut Hystérie,
Parlez Pistache, and Mon Petit Kumquat.

697
Martine's Chocolates

—⚮—

The delightful chocolate aroma that greets you as you enter
New York City's Bloomingdale's is probably from Martine's, made right on site.
Each shape contains a different center. Made with fresh American cream
and French butter, these chocolates must be eaten
within 5 days of purchase.

698

L.A. Burdick

L. A. Burdick Chocolates
Walpole, N.H.

Larry Burdick began making chocolates in the 1990s in New York City for several fine restaurants and caterers. Now based in Walpole, New Hampshire, the refined chocolates are delivered weekly to New York City customers and shipped internationally. Burdick also makes a signature chocolate mouse: hand-piped chocolate ganache forms the body and the ears are made from almonds. The mice come in milk, white, and dark chocolate; all of them have silk tails. Adorable penguins have chocolate ganache bodies and almond flippers.

699
Li-Lac Chocolates

A Greenwich Village institution since 1923, this chocolate shop is touted for its extraordinary chocolate with old world charm. Peanut Raisin Clusters, Caramel Squares, Chocolate-Covered Ginger, and Butter Crunch along with an assortment of truffles, are some of the shop's specialties.

700
Knipschildt

Based in Norwalk, Connecticut, this chocolate company uses Valrhona and Michel Cluizel chocolates to make their truffles, which come in a variety of decadent flavors, including lavender, caramel, lemon, champagne, mocha, and amaretto.

701
Garrison Confections

It was while Andrew Shotts was working as the pastry chef at La Côte Basque in New York City that he dreamed of having his own artisanal line of chocolates. Today, Garrison Confections is housed in the historic Providence, Rhode Island, Biltmore Hotel. Customers seek out Shotts's peanut butter patties, coconut patties, and coffee hazelnut tablets.

702
MarieBelle

Since 2000, Founder Maribel Lieberman
of New York City's SoHo has created chocolates that
look like miniature works of art packed in her signature
blue-and-brown boxes. For a special gift, they offer a
chocolate-filled red leather trunk, as well as chocolate
bars decorated with vintage labels of pin-up girls
for every month of the year.

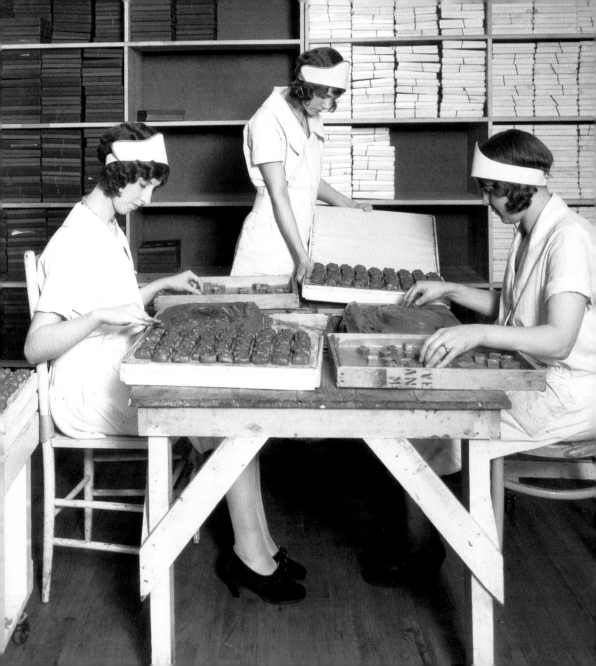

703
Black Hound

―◦◦◦―

New York City chocolate lovers recognize the beribboned, Shaker-style,
wooden boxes lined with tissue paper and holding rich truffles. In addition
to truffles, Black Hound is also known for its cakes and cookies. The Chocolate
Pyramid is filled with layers of bittersweet chocolate with Gran Marnier,
milk chocolate with Framboise, and white chocolate with Calvados.
The entire creation is surrounded by a luxurious coating
of Belgian chocolate and a dusting of cocoa powder.

704
Payard

―◦◦◦―

Based in Manhattan; Manhasset, New York; and Brazil, Payard is known
for their pastries, wedding cakes, and chocolates. Their Mint Julep Cup
is a stylish silver cup filled with 24 truffles made of dark
chocolate ganache with a hint of rum and then lightly
dusted with cocoa powder. They have an assortment
of truffles with French-inspired names such as
the Louvre, Notre Dame and Vendome.

705 *Harbor Sweets*

Sweet Sloops, the company's signature chocolate, is a sail[
shaped piece of almond crunch covered in white choc[
and then dipped in dark chocolate and crushed pe[
Based in Salem, Massachusetts, Harbor Sweets was foun[
in 1973 by Ben Strohecker and today is run by Phyllis
LeBlanc, who had been a part-time candy
dipper at the store while she was a college
student 25 years ago.

HARBOR SWEETS

Gift Assortment
24 handmade chocolates
8 1/4 oz.(233g)

710
Ethel M

Located 5 miles from the Las Vegas strip, Ethel M offers a tour
of its candy-making factory. Almond Butter Krisps and Satin Cremes
(including raspberry and lemon) are some of Ethel M's signature chocolates.
Besides making chocolate, the company recycles the 32,000 gallons
of water they use each day for landscaping purposes.

711
Stephany's Chocolates

Founded in 1963 in Denver following old-world candy-making traditions,
Stephany's has grown to include several Denver area shops. Creators of the
Denver Mint, a hand-poured confection with 3 layers of chocolate flavored with
triple-distilled peppermint oil, Stephany's is also known for
their award-winning Colorado Almond Toffee.

712
Scharffen Berger Chocolate Maker

—⁓⁓⁓—

This Berkeley, California, chocolate maker, founded in 1996
by longtime friends Robert Steinberg—a physician with a superb palette
—and John Scharffenberger, uses restored vintage European machinery
to make a flavorful dark chocolate of the highest quality. The secret
to their success is careful bean selection, blending, roasting,
and conching, as well as the special care they take
with small-batch processing.

713
Guittard

—⁓⁓⁓—

During the gold rush of the mid-1800s, Etienne Guittard
journeyed to the Barbary Coast in hopes of discovering gold. While he
did not discover gold, on his way back he did bring back chocolate from his
uncle's factory in France and established the Guittard Chocolate Factory
in San Francisco in 1868. Today Guittard chocolate, whether it
be bars or chips for homemade cookies, is used by discerning
professionals and home bakers alike.

714
Sterling Truffle Bar

Triangular-shaped bars of chocolate are the signature of this northern California chocolate company. Vibrant colors and contemporary designs as well as enticing flavors that include pineapple ginger macadamia nut, double hazelnut caramel, and rocky road are just a few of the flavor choices.

715
Joseph Schmidt

Started in 1983 in a tucked-away neighborhood in San Francisco, Joseph Schmidt, a European-trained baker, and his partner opened their first and only shop and soon began to focus on their chocolate creations. A box of Schmidt's signature egg-shaped truffles is immediately recognized and welcomed by many chocolate lovers.

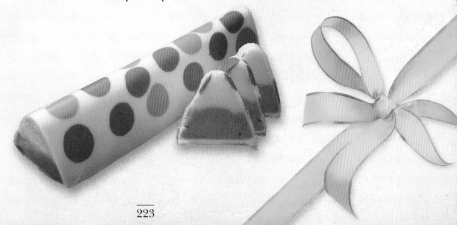

716
Mary's Japan

~~~

Founded 53 years ago in Tokyo, Mary's offers a selection
with an East-West theme. Some of their chocolates include Japanese Plum
(fresh plum liqueur blended with bittersweet ganache) and Lily of the Valley
(with a green tea-flavored ganache filling). Graceful chocolate flowers are
piped on the surface. Japanese truffles include Purple Sweet Potato,
Golden Sesame, Kinako Soybean Flour, and Bean Paste.

717
See's Candies

~~~

Charles See founded this beloved chocolate company in 1921,
using his mother's recipes. Mary See's smiling face still decorates boxes
of these candies today, which are available throughout the West. With over 100
varieties of chocolate, one can sit down with a box and enjoy many
different types before running into a repeat.

718
Michel Cluizel

~∘∘~

Chocolatier Michel Cluizel makes superb quality dark and milk varietal chocolates from select plantations. For instance, the Grand Cru is made from single-origin cocoa beans from the Barlovento Valley in Venezuela.

719
XOX *Truffles*

~∘∘~

Don't be fooled by the stony countenances of these jagged-edged truffles—they have been ranked by many chocolate professionals as some of the most delicious in the world. Some of the flavors from this San Francisco–based company include framboise, amaretto, rum coco, and liqueur de noisette.

720
Chuao

Named after the prestigious cacao-producing area of Chuao in central Venezuela, this Encinitas, California, company uses Venezuelan chocolate and traditional European techniques. One of their more unique chocolates is the Picante, which is made with California raisins and Valley cabernet caramel with a hint of pasilla chili and cayenne pepper for a bit of heat. Then the pieces are drenched in dark chocolate.

721
El Rey

One of the oldest chocolate producers in Venezuela, this company is known for selecting quality beans and producing chocolates with a higher quantity of cocoa butter, which means their chocolate is able to form a thinner shell than other chocolates.

Organic Chocolate:
Good for Planet Earth

722
Newman's Own Organics

※

Nell Newman, daughter of Paul Newman, created a spin-off line of organic products, which features Milk Chocolate, Sweet Dark Chocolate, Butter Toffee Crunch, Milk Chocolate Crisp Rice, Sweet Dark Chocolate Orange, and Sweet Dark Chocolate Espresso bars, as well as cookies and peanut butter cups.

723
Yachana Jungle Chocolate

※

Made from Fair Trade Federation–approved cacao that earns Ecuadorian farmers 200% to 300% above the local market price. It's completely unprocessed (without milk, butter, sugar, or other ingredients) and will not melt or spoil.

724
Dagoba

※

This Oregon-based company produces Chaicolate; lime, roseberry, chocolatte, and Brasilia flavors, among many others.

725
Green & Black

With a very high cocoa content,
Green & Black's cocoa beans are certified
organic and grown under the shade of
indigenous rainforest trees in the Dominican
Republic and Belize. In addition to making
chocolate bars, the company produces luxury
chocolate gift items, many flavors of ice cream,
and Hazelnut Chocolate Butter—
perfect for slathering on your
favorite organic bread.

726
Cloud Nine

Founded in 1991, Cloud Nine
is committed to making "politically correct,
adult candy bars," some of them totally organic:
Green Tea Crisp, Hazelnut Crunch, and Java
Roast. They donate 10% of their annual
profits to rainforest preservation and
to protecting indigenous people.

Hawaii

727

The Big Island of Hawaii is the only place
in the United States that produces cocoa,
making Hawaii the only location in the world
where the raw ingredients for the three
major infusion beverages—coffee,
tea, and cacao—are grown.

728

Unlike other chocolate manufacturers
in the United States that use cocoa imported
from overseas, Hawaiian chocolates are made
completely from locally grown products.

729
Big Island Candies

Established in 1977, Big Island Candies' main focus is the production
of premium macadamia nut chocolates and cookies.

730
Hawaiian Vintage Chocolate

Manufacturers of the chocolate that has the distinction of being the brand Bill Gates chose to serve at his wedding and the one the Dalai Lama selected for his first taste of chocolate ever. HVC ages their cocoa beans for one year before processing.

731
Wow-Wee Maui

Manufacturers of Wow-Wee Maui candy bars in 6 unique varieties. You can choose from milk chocolate, dark chocolate or white chocolate combined with Hawaiian specialties such as macadamia nuts, kona coffee, chewy banana, and caramel.

732
The Kailua Candy Company

Kailua Candy Company specializes in chocolate infused with a swirl of kona coffee, and macadamia nut Honas (Hawaiian for turtles). They also carry a unique line of "edible art" — carvings of island scenes made of rich dark chocolate.

Mexico

733 Traditional Mexican chocolate, made by grinding together cinnamon sticks, cocoa beans, and almonds, is different from any other chocolate in the world.

734 Mexican chocolate is made without conching, the slow kneading process that produces a smooth texture. In Mexico, most chocolate is produced to make hot chocolate or mole.

735 70% of the cocoa beans grown in Mexico are from the state of Tabasco; the other 30% are grown in Chiapas.

736 The heart of Mexican chocolate production is Oaxaca, home of 3 of the country's largest chocolate manufacturers and over 115 chocolate grinders.

737 Mexican hot chocolate is always served with a cap of foam (*espumo*) on top that is said to embody the spirit of the chocolate and the energy of the person who prepared it.

738 In rural Mexico, a woman's worth as a cook is often judged by the amount of foam she can create on a cup of hot chocolate.

739 During the Day of the Dead celebration in Mexico, from October 31st thru November 2nd, family members remember the dead with offerings of chocolate.

740 In Mexico, when asking for a woman's hand in marriage, the suitor brings chocolate to her family.

741 After the birth of a child, Mexican parents pass out chocolate to their family and friends.

742 Piñatas at Mexican children's birthday parties are filled with chocolates.

743 Chocolate is also given out at baptisms, first communions, weddings, and funerals.

744 Chorrote

A Tabascan drink made with fresh cocoa beans, corn, sugar, and water.

745 Champurrado

A chocolate-flavored, corn-based beverage.

746 Chocolate Atole

A porridge-like drink with a cap of chocolate foam on top.

747 Jugo de Cacao

A drink made with sweetened fresh cocoa.

748 Tejate

A cold drink made of dark chocolate, corn masa, and flower petals.

749
Mexican chocolate brands,
available in the United States: Ibarra,
La Abuelita, Popular.

750
Chocolates Mayordomo
One of several mills owned by the Concha
family, this is the largest chocolate
manufacturer in Oaxaca City.

751
Chocolates Guelaguetza
A family owned company founded in 1958
that produces a powdered chocolate drink
called Choco Punch.

752
Chocolates La Soledad
Specializes in chocolates filled with mezcal.

—◦◦◦—

*Las cosas claras y
el chocolate espeso.
(Ideas should be clear
and chocolate thick.)*

—Spanish proverb

Those who have been

too long at their labor,

who have drunk too long

at the cup of voluptuousness,

who feel they have become

temporarily inhumane,

who are tormented by

their families, who find life

sad and love ephemeral;

they should all eat

chocolate and they

will be comforted.

—Jean Anthelme Brillat-Savarin, b. 1755,
  French jurist and gastronome

Chocolate Nations

Citizens of these countries really love chocolate, as their average annual consumption (in pounds per year) makes clear.

753 Switzerland (22.36)

754 Austria (20.13)

755 Ireland (19.47)

756 Germany (18.04)

757 Norway (17.93)

758 Denmark (17.66)

759 United Kingdom (17.49)

760 Belgium (13.16)

761 Australia (12.99)

762 Sweden (12.90)

763 United States (11.64)

764 France (11.38)

765
Milk chocolate is to Switzerland
what champagne is to France.

Switzerland

766

The people of Switzerland consume about 22 pounds of chocolate a year per person, leading the world in per capita chocolate consumption.

767

Chocolat.tv is a Web TV channel with a purple-spotted cow as its mascot. The channel even runs a soap opera starring a cow named Violette.

768

The Swiss Chocolate Train departs from Montreux once a week from June through October. After a stop in the medieval cheese-making town of Gruyères, the train takes passengers to Broc, the home of the Cailler-Nestlé chocolate factory, for a tour and chocolate sampling. After you have had your fill of chocolates, the train returns to Montreux.

769
Café Schober

Located in Old Town, one of the most picturesque parts of Zurich,
this pastry and chocolate shop is usually decorated with hundreds of flowers.
Popular choices are kugelhopf and the shop's hot chocolate, which is made from
the thick creamy milk produced by the café's own herd of Brown Swiss cows.

770
Confiserie Sprungli

The company traces its origins to a tiny confectioner's shop
that first opened in 1720. By 1836, it became Sprungli Confectioner's.
(This was also the very beginning of the Lindt & Sprungli company.) Today there
are several locations in Zurich, which showcase decadent displays of pastries
and chocolate desserts, including their famous Luxemburgerli macaroons
filled with fine buttercream in an assortment of flavors
including chocolate, mocha, hazelnut,
raspberry, lemon, and caramel.

771
Confiserie Honold

—∞—

This Zurich-based shop, with its cozy back tea room, is the perfect place for a coffee and chocolate pick-me-up.

772
Teuscher

—∞—

Over 60 years ago in a small town in the Swiss Alps, Dolf Teuscher, a master chocolate maker, started his premium chocolate-making business. Today, the Teuscher kitchen in Zurich makes more than 100 varieties of chocolates using the original family recipes. The candies are prepared each week and flown to stores in America, Canada, and Asia. Teuscher is probably most famous for their champagne truffles, a blend of fresh cream, butter, and chocolate with a champagne cream center, and dusted with confectioners' sugar.

773
Lindt & Sprungli

David Sprungli-Schwarz and his son,
Rudolf Sprungli-Ammann, founded a small confectionary
shop in Zurich in 1845. Producing chocolate in its solid form
made them very popular and successful in this land of chocolate lovers.
As the business grew, the Sprungli heirs joined forces with the famous
Berne chocolate factory of Rodolphe Lindt, who was famous for inventing
the conchage technique in 1879. American home cooks still use their
satiny smooth bars for baking (when they're not snacking on them).
And it's tough to choose just one piece from a box
of colorfully-wrapped Lindor Truffles.

The 12-step
chocoholics program:
Never be more
than 12 steps away
from chocolate.

—Terry Moore

France

―∞∞∞―

774

Club des Croqueurs de Chocolat (Club of Chocolate Munchers),
an exclusive group of French chocolate connoisseurs who meet four times a year,
taste new creations from famous chocolatiers, and vote their approval
or disapproval with a show of hands.

775

Lenôtre, famous in Paris for his gateau opera and meringue-and-chocolate
mousse-filled condorede.

776

Dalloyau, an aristocratic tea salon, perfectly suited
for people-watching and enjoying a cup of tea with cake mogador
(chocolate cake with chocolate mousse and raspberry jam).

777

Angelina, known for its Africain, a rich hot chocolate
made from melted chocolate bars.

778

Pain au chocolat in Paris, eaten while strolling through
Left Bank neighborhoods.

779

The dessert section at Fauchon in Paris.

780
Maison du Chocolat

———

Owner Robert Linxe is the undisputed king of chocolate.
Each diminutive chocolate is a carefully hand-crafted miniature work of art.
One of the chocolates he is known for is the Romeo — a light milk chocolate
mousse is combined with fresh, very finely filtered mocha coffee, and then coated
with a dark chocolate couverture. Linxe says, "In this way, I obtain a subtle,
velvety smooth penetrating aroma, particularly sensual and seductive.
It is well tuned to the character of Romeo,
the great lover of legend."

781
Christian Constant

—◦◦◦—

*Paris chocolatier Constant uses criollo beans from the islands
of the Indian Ocean, cinnamon and tea from Ceylon, cardamom
from Malabar, and vanilla from Raiatea (near Tahiti).*

782
Richart

—◦◦◦—

*In addition to the Paris flagship store, Richart has boutiques
in Spain, Sweden, Japan, and the United States. Petits Richart
are tiny but burst with flavor.*

783
Valrhona

—◦◦◦—

*Used by some of the finest professional chocolatiers
and pastry makers in the world, it is also available
to the home cook through specialty food stores.
Valrhona makes several varieties of chocolate;
Araguani boasts a level of 72% cocoa,
a very intense chocolate experience.*

784
Mazet

⌐∾∾⌐

A century after its founding
in the French village of Montargis,
Mazet is still creating deluxe chocolates
in stylish partitioned boxes featuring varieties
of chocolate pralines, 9 different ganaches,
chocolate citrus peels, and caramelized nuts,
as well as their unique and popular
fondue in 7 flavors.

85 Chocolate Mousse

erve this mousse in stemmed wine glasses. Garnish
ach serving with a few raspberries and a sprig of
hint, or a dollop of sweetened whipped cream and
few chocolate curls.

ounces bittersweet chocolate, broken into pieces
1/2 cup milk
Pinch of salt
1 tablespoon vegetable oil
1 tablespoon black raspberry liqueur (such as
     Chambord), orange-flavored liqueur (such as
     Gran Marnier, Cointreau or Triple Sec), or cognac
1 1/2 teaspoons vanilla extract
1 cup heavy (whipping) cream, chilled

Chill a large bowl. Place the chocolate in the container
of a food processor fitted with the metal blade and
process for 20 to 30 seconds, or until the chocolate
is finely chopped.

Place the milk and salt in a small saucepan over
medium heat and cook, stirring occasionally with a
wooden spoon, until the mixture just comes to a boil.
Remove the pan from the heat.

With the motor of the food processor running, pour
the hot milk through the feed tube. Process for 10 to

20 seconds, or until the chocolate is completely
melted. Add the oil, liqueur, and vanilla and
process for another 5 to 10 seconds, or until the
mixture is combined. Scrape the mixture into
a large bowl and let cool for 20 to 30 minutes.

Place the cream in the chilled bowl, and using
a hand-held electric mixer, beat the cream
until peaks just start to form.

Using a rubber spatula, gently fold one-third
of the whipped cream into the chocolate
mixture to lighten it. Fold in the remaining
whipped cream until just combined.

Spoon the mixture into 4 stemmed dessert
glasses or wine glasses. Cover the glasses
with plastic wrap and refrigerate for 1 to
2 hours, or until the mixture is set. The
mousse may be prepared up to 2 days
in advance.

Makes 4 servings

Belgium

786 History and trends show that if a chocolatier can make it in Belgium, he or she can probably make it anywhere in the world.

787 There are 2,130 chocolate shops in the country. Even the smallest villages generally have at least one shop.

788 Filled chocolates in Belgium are called pralines, which should not be confused with the American praline, a confection made of nuts and brown sugar.

789 Museum Temple of Chocolate Cote D'Or

790 Musée du Chocolat Jacques

791 Musée du Cacao et du Chocolat

792 Musée de la Patisserie

793 La Fonderie, a guided chocolate factory tour in Brussels

794 Chocolate World, a shop in Antwerp, has everything a baker could want, including chocolate molds in almost unlimited shapes and sizes. The store will even create a chocolate mold of your own design.

795 Belgium produces 172,000 tons of chocolate per year.

796
Le Chocolatier Manon

— ∞ —

Made with luscious cream from Belgian cows, totally handmade, hand-molded, and hand-dipped, this Brussels chocolatier is famous for its double interiors and for its distinctively-shaped "sputniks": a crisp chocolate cup filled with crème fraîche and topped with a cone of bittersweet orange buttercream and almond paste, then dipped in chocolate and sprinkled with 14-carat gold.

797
Wittamer

— ∞ —

A favorite since 1910, this Brussels chocolatier is known for the Trianon, an architectural confection of nougatine on a base of ganache. The Bouchon is a chocolate champagne cork filled with Gran Marnier cream.

798
Mary Chocolatier

— ∞ —

Founded in 1919, this Brussels chocolatier offers over 60 different varieties of sophisticated dark chocolate and a multitude of delectable fillings, including dark chocolate mousse in 5 distinct degrees of bitterness.

799
Neuhaus

Founded in 1857 in Brussels by Swiss immigrant Jean Neuhaus and his son Frederic, the company began as a pharmaceutical confectionery company. Father and son soon left pharmaceuticals behind; the company invented the filled chocolate, or praline, in 1912. Today, 2400 tons of Neuhaus chocolates are sold annually in 50 countries.

800
Galler

One of the most unusual specialties offered at this shop is their "cat's tongues," cartoon cats molded from chocolate. Cat's tongues come in 4 flavors: Praline Lait, Noir Extreme, Blanc Praline, and Praline Fondant. There are more than 2,000 sales outlets and 17 Galler stores in Belgium alone.

801
Leonidas

While American confectioner Leonidas Kestekides was visiting Belgium for the 1910 World's Fair, he met and married a Belgian woman, settled in Brussels, and created many inspired chocolates. Leonidas designed shops where passersby could see the chocolates that were for sale and then reach through a window to buy them.

802
Godiva

—❧—

Master chocolatier Joseph Draps founded Godiva
in 1926 in Brussels. Named for the legend of Lady Godiva,
the company's chocolates are also legendary. Godiva was a major
force in introducing Americans to premium quality, European-style
chocolates. Godiva's shell-molded chocolates are sold in signature
gold ballotins. The company also produces chocolate-flavored
concoctions such as Godiva Liqueur, ultra-premium
ice cream, and cookies.

803
Pierre Marcolini

—❧—

After a childhood of hoarding chocolate,
Pierre and his wife Nicolette opened their first chocolate
shop in Brussels. Today they have 12 shops around the world.
Marcolini's pralines are made from dark, milk, and white chocolate
and include exotic fillings such as ganache with jasmine tea
and a lemon-and-lime fondant filling. For discerning
chocolate lovers, they offer Palets fins—
small cubes of chocolate made from
single-origin criolla beans.

Chocolate Museums

—◦◦◦◦—

You can tour the world and visit a chocolate museum everywhere you go. Most museums tell the bean-to-bar story of how chocolate is made. Many are sponsored or run by chocolate companies. The best part is the chocolate samples that often complete the tour.

Austria

804
Walter Heindl Museum, Vienna

Belgium

805
Musée du Cacao et du Chocolat, Brussels

Brazil

806
Prawer Museum of Chocolate

Canada

807
Erico Choco Museum, Quebec

808
Ganong Chocolate Museum, St. Stephane

Great Britain

818
Cadbury World, Birmingham

Hungary

819
Csokoladé Museum, Budapest

Italy

820
Museo del Cioccolato Antica Norba, Norma

Japan

821
Ishiya Chocolate Museum, Sapporo

Korea

822
Chocolate Museum, Jeju-do

Netherlands

823
Chocolade Museum, Amsterdam

Russia

824
Krasny Oktyabr Museum, Moscow

Spain

825
Museo Xocolata, Barcelona

826
Museo Valor, Villajoyosa

827
Museo del Chocolate, Astorga

Switzerland

828
Alprose Museum of Chocolate, Caslano-Lugano

829
Cailler-Nestlé Museum, Broc

Germany

830

When chocolate first appeared in Germany at the end of the 17th century,
Frederick I of Prussia imposed a tax on it. Anyone wishing to partake
in the pleasure of hot chocolate had to pay 2 thalers.

831

In 1792 the Josty brothers opened a confectioner's shop in Berlin
that made Swiss chocolate available to the German people. It was such a success
that they opened a chocolate factory shortly after.

832
Chocolatier Hachez

Established in 1890, this company has produced exclusive, cocoa-rich chocolate specialties based on original recipes from Joseph Emile Hachez. Today Chocolatier Hachez is a synonym for dark chocolate specialties.

833
Storz

Founded in 1884 by Christian Storz, who was a renowned confectioner of the time, the company survived both world wars. Today Storz produces a variety of specialty chocolates, including an entire line of Flying Chocolates, chocolates shaped like anything that flies, from airplanes to ladybug, and Fantasy Chocolates, which come in a variety of unusual shapes.

834
Gina

Founded in 1911 by George Woltersdorf, who named the company after his daughter, Gina specializes solely in the production of chocolate coins. Over 5,000 international currencies are available.

835
Alfred Ritter

~~~

Manufacturer of the Ritter Sport line of chocolate products.

836
Feodora Chocolate

~~~

Established in 1910, Feodora is a family-owned chocolate company
that was given its name by Princess Feodora, the sister of the last empress
of Germany. According to the story, the princess was so moved by the quality
and taste of the family's chocolate that she appointed them to use
her name and signature as their logo.

Italy

837 Italy was the second European country, after Spain, to discover the exotic beverage, hot chocolate, in the mid 1600s.

838 Chocolate arrived in Switzerland when Italians from the border-town of Ticino, introduced it to their Swiss neighbors toward the end of the 1600s.

839 Eurochocolate Perugia is an annual 9-day festival that transforms Perugia into a huge open-air pastry shop. The streets are filled with vendors selling every imaginable delight for chocolate enthusiasts.

840 Turin, known as the chocolate capital of Italy, holds a month-long Cioccolato Fair, in which local artists compete for the spotlight by creating confectionary recreations of everything from Turin's landmarks, to three-foot-high airplanes, to a full-sized milk chocolate replica of a wedding feast.

841 The Italian treat, Gianduja (hazelnut-flavored chocolate) was invented in Turin during the Napoleonic wars, when local hazelnuts were used to compensate for cocoa shortages. Nutella, the commercial version invented after World War II by the chocolatiers Ferrero.

842 Piemontese Tonda Gentile hazelnuts, used to make Gianduja, have been granted "protected geographical indication" status by the European Union—equivalent to the stamp of approval given to wines in order to distinguish original products from inferior copies.

Italian Easter Eggs

In Italy, unlike America, Easter isn't synonymous with baskets
full of chocolate bunnies and marshmallow chicks. Easter displays in Italian bars,
supermarkets, pastry shops, and especially chocolate shops, are comprised of brightly wrapped
uova di Pasqua—chocolate Easter eggs. Made mostly of milk chocolate, the eggs range in size
from 1/3 ounce to 18 pounds, and all but the very smallest contain a treat inside such as
a little silver picture frame or gold-dipped costume jewelry. The very best eggs are
handmade by artisans who allow the purchaser to supply their own surprise
—car keys, engagement rings, and watches have all been tucked
into Italian chocolate eggs.

843
Laboratorio Artigianale del Giandujotto

One of the top choices for uova di Pasqua, this shop produces fine classic
Giandujotto chocolate. Silky smooth chocolate made from house-roasted cocoa
is mixed with top-quality, finely-ground Piemontese hazelnuts to produce
exquisite, foil-wrapped morsels that melt in your mouth.

844
Dolgam Industria Dolciaria

Founded in the small mountain town of Nunziata by the Gangemi brothers,
this confectionary has been in operation for over 40 years. Specialties of the house
are gourmet uova di Pasqua and a wide selection of typical Sicilian torroncini.

Easter

~≈~

845 More than 60 million chocolate bunnies are produced for Easter.

846 Foil-wrapped, solid milk chocolate eggs in plastic, egg-shaped containers

847 A whole bag of malted milk chocolate eggs to eat

848 Your very own chocolate Easter bunny— especially if it is solid chocolate

849 Trying to decide what part of the bunny to eat first

850 The cute candy eye on your chocolate bunny, which brings him to life

851 Biting the ears off

852 Nibbling the feet

853
Amedei of Tuscany

Founded by the brother and sister team of Cecilia and Alessio Tessieri in 1990, Amedei is considered to produce some of the finest chocolate in the world. Amedei has gained world exclusive rights to the infamous Chuao plantation in Venezuela. Amedei differs from many chocolate makers because they process the cocoa themselves, resulting in a unique aromatic and extra-smooth chocolate.

854
Cuba Venchi

Cuba Venchi is the product of a marriage between two traditional chocolatiers from Italy's Piedmont region. Venchi had its start as a fine chocolate company in 1878, while Cuba (Cussino, Biscotti e Affini) arrived on the scene in 1949. The two companies merged in 2000, and Cuba Venchi is known for producing some of the best Italian chocolate using only pure, natural ingredients.

855
Caffarel

When Pierre Paul Caffarel opened the doors of his chocolate shop in Turin over 175 years ago, he purchased a unique industrial machine capable of producing 705 pounds of chocolate a day. Known the world over as the very first company to create gianduija, today Caffarel enjoys the undisputed reputation of creating Italy's finest chocolate.

856
Ferrero

In the 1940s Pietro Ferrero founded his chocolate company on the desire to create premium candy at affordable prices. Ferrero is the world's third largest confectionary company today. Their most famous products—Rocher and Nutella—are sold around the globe, and the company has state-of-the-art manufacturing facilities throughout Europe, North America, Australia, and South America.

FERRERO ROCHER

FERRERO

There were three methods of coating centers with chocolate: hand dipping, enrobing, and molding. Hand dipping was the oldest and, of course, required the least investment in equipment. All you needed was a container—pot, kettle or saucepan—which would melt the chocolate and keep it melted while you picked up a center, swished it around in the melted chocolate, set it down on a tray, used a finger to make a little chocolate string or other shape on top of the coated piece, to identify the center, and left it to cool and harden.

Enrobing was the coating method used by most candy companies in the United States. It involved placing the centers on a mesh conveyor belt and running the conveyor through a shower bath of molten chocolate. Excess chocolate fell through the mesh and was pumped back up to shower again. This left the bottom of the piece uncoated, so after the shower bath, the mesh conveyor carried the piece through a "bottomer," which was a puddle of chocolate on the path of the conveyer. The piece then moved past a group of workers who put the identifying string on the top and then went through a refrigerated cooling tunnel where it hardened. At the other end, the conveyor (now canvas or rubber rather than metal mesh) carried the finished pieces past the packers, who removed them by hand into stock boxes for storage until needed to make up an assortment in a finished box.

European chocolate makers (Godiva, for one) commonly used the molding method of coating, which involved placing or pumping the center into a metal mold of the proper size and shape, filling the rest of the space with molten chocolate, letting it all set, and knocking out the finished pieces.

—Samuel R. Kostick, former Vice President, Loft Candy

Chocolate ...

857

is an anywhere, anytime treat

858

comes in all sizes

859

is always age-appropriate

860

never goes out of style

861

can be naughty or nice

862

even a thin coating smoothes out
the wrinkles in raisins

Growing Up With Chocolate

863 At summer camp, spending your last canteen money on a chocolate bar

864 Blaming your acne on chocolate

865 Sharing a hot fudge sundae with your first love

866 Getting over a broken heart with your best friend and a giant bag of M&M's

867 Baking a heart-shaped chocolate cake for your valentine

868 Fueling a sleepover with Twix, Snickers, Baby Ruths, and Three Musketeers

869 Sharing a chocolate care package from home with your dorm mates

870 Bringing back chocolate treats from foreign study trips for your friends at home

871 During finals, making a 3 a.m. convenience store run for something—anything!—chocolate

872 Hershey's® "Perfectly Chocolate" Chocolate Cake

Here's a wonderful choice for your favorite chocolate lover's birthday cake!

2 cups sugar
1 3/4 cups all-purpose flour, plus more for the pans
3/4 cup Hershey's® Cocoa
1-1/2 teaspoons baking powder
1-1/2 teaspoons baking soda

1 teaspoon salt
2 eggs
1 cup milk
1/2 cup vegetable oil, plus more for the pans
2 teaspoons vanilla extract
1 cup boiling water

Preheat the oven to 350°F. Grease and flour two 9-inch round baking pans.

Stir together the sugar, flour, cocoa, baking powder, baking soda and salt in the bowl of a standing mixer. Add the eggs, milk, oil, and vanilla and beat on medium speed for 2 minutes. Stir in the boiling water (the batter will be thin). Pour the batter into the prepared pans.

Bake for 30 to 35 minutes, or until a wooden toothpick inserted in the center comes out clean. Cool 10 minutes; remove from the pans to wire racks and cool completely.

Frost with "Perfectly Chocolate" Chocolate Frosting (recipe follows).

Makes 10 to 12 servings.

873 Hershey's® "Perfectly Chocolate" Chocolate Frosting

1 stick (1/2 cup) unsalted butter or margarine
2/3 cup Hershey's Cocoa
3 cups powdered sugar
1/3 cup milk
1 teaspoon vanilla extract

Place the butter in a large microwavable bowl and microwave for 2 minutes, or until the butter is melted. Stir in the cocoa. Alternately add the powdered sugar and the milk, beating to reach a spreading consistency. Add a little more milk if needed. Stir in the vanilla.

Makes about 2 cups of frosting

Chocolate on the Silver Screen

874 ***Bread and Chocolate
(Pane e Cioccolata)*** **(1973)**
An Italian immigrant tries to fit into Swiss society, but fails.
He refuses to give up hope in the face of adversity.

875 ***Like Water for Chocolate
(Como Agua para Chocolate)*** **(1992)**
A story of forbidden love. When Tita's mother refuses to
allow her to marry her beloved Pedro, Tita channels her
passion and grief into her cooking.

876 ***Chocolat*** **(2000)**
A single mother and her daughter move to a small French
village and open a chocolate shop. The town's propriety
is shaken.

877 ***Willy Wonka & the Chocolate Factory*** **(1971)**
When reclusive chocolate factory owner Willy Wonka
announces a contest in which five winners will receive a
tour of the factory, a poor boy named Charlie miraculously
comes up a winner.

878
The Chocolate Soldier (1941)
A musical comedy about a husband-and-wife singing duo from Vienna. When Karl decides to test his wife' fidelity, he poses as a Russian soldier and attempts t seduce her, but is only left confused.

879
The Chocolate War (1988)
One boy's quest for personal freedom as an idealistic freshman at a Catholic high school. After being forced into selling chocolates for the school's annual fundraiser, a sadistic headmaster, and a gang of bully classmates make the boy's life hell when he decides he won't be pushed around anymore.

880
Down With Love (2003)
Author Barbara Novak advises women to forget about romance and work on their careers. She suggests that if they feel the stirrings of love, they should eat chocolate instead.

881
E.T. the Extra-Terrestrial (1982)
An extra-terrestrial gets left behind and befriends a boy and his family. Among the many lessons he learns about human life, the most memorable is the joy of Reese's Pieces.

882
My Fair Lady (1964)
A professor of languages and a visiting colleague make a bet as whether or not a "commoner" can be transformed into a beautiful lady. In the film, a box of chocolates is symbolic of everything that goes with the "good life."

883
Forrest Gump (1994)
A sweet-natured, simple man from Alabama encounters many luminaries during his life, including Elvis Presley, John Lennon, and JFK. Of the many adages to come out of the film, "Life is like a box of chocolates" is one of the most frequently quoted.

Chocolate Movie Snacks

884
Goobers

885
Raisinets

886
Bon Bons

887
Whoppers

888
Buncha Crunch

889
Charleston
Chew

890
Cookie Dough
Bites

891
Junior Mints

892
Milk Duds

893
Muddy Bears

894
Sno-Caps

895 Chocolate Labradors

Things That Remind Us of Chocolate

896 Weimaraners

897 Chocolate Poodles

898 Raw Sienna Crayola Crayons

899 Sepia Crayola Crayons

900 Brown suede Ferragamo shoes

901 Natural mink coats

902 Silk, cashmere, and pearls

903 Cocoa butter cosmetics

904 Brown University

905 UPS uniforms

Chocolate Molds

906 The first antique chocolate molds were made in France in 1820.

907 The German company Anton Reiche has made more than 50,000 different designs for chocolate molds.

908 Plastic chocolate molds effectively replaced metal molds around 1960. The old and lovely chocolate molds are still used, however, for beeswax and soap as well as chocolate.

909 While pouring tempered chocolate into a clean, dry mold, and gently tap the mold to remove air bubbles. Tap the mold again after it is filled.

910 Refrigerate the filled mold until cool, then release the chocolate from the mold.

911

A favorite chocolate cream cheese cupcake recipe that you bake for your college roommate and send to her on her birthday, and she does the same for you on your birthday.

912

The way super dark chocolate explodes across your taste buds, slightly sour and tangy across the back of the tongue. Just a small piece feels rich and satisfying.

913

The way coarsely chopped chocolate almost magically becomes shiny and smooth when it melts.

Christmas

914 The biggest period for boxed chocolate sales occurs during the winter holidays—the time period between Thanksgiving and New Year's Day.

915 Chocolates wrapped as "lumps of coal" in your Christmas stocking

916 Fudge and chocolate-dipped cookies on the cookie trays

917 Drinking hot chocolate while you are opening gifts

918 Watching the "Hot Chocolate" ballet during the annual production of *The Nutcracker*

919 150 million chocolate Santas of all sizes are produced each year.

920 A chocolate Santa—even better if it's solid chocolate

921
Chocolate Cosmos
(*Cosmos atrosanguineus*),
with velvety dark maroon
flowers and a faint scent
of chocolate.

The Chocolate Garden

Yes, it's possible. Not only the color, but also the scent of chocolate will intoxicate anyone who plants this garden.

922 Hot Cocoa Rose, with clusters of rusty chocolate, cinnamon-ruffled blooms

923 Chocolate Beauty Pepper *(Capsicum annuum)*, with chocolate-colored peppers that are sweet and delicious

924 Chocolate Chip Bugleweed *(Ajuga)*, an evergreen groundcover with small, narrow, chocolate-colored leaves and blue flower spikes

925 Fiveleaf Akebia *(Akebia quinata)*, an extremely tough evergreen that produces chocolate-colored flowers in the early summer

926 Black Magic Rose Geranium, a hybrid geranium with dark, chocolate-colored leaf centers and green edges

927 Common Sweetshrub *(Calycanthus floridus)*, a shrub with dark, ribbon-like petals the color of cinnamon-spiced chocolate

928 Cocoa shells as a fine, aromatic mulch

Biggest, Oddest Chocolates

929
The Holy Koran

69 inches high by 99 inches wide, modeled in 740 pounds
of white chocolate by Indonesian chef Agus Roba'i.

930
Vladimir Putin

The Russian president, in a chocolate-painted portrait on a 3.3-pound slab
of solid chocolate, created by the Moscow chocolate-maker Konfael.

931
Chocolate Chip Cookie

The world's largest, baked on May 17, 2003, by the Immaculate Baking Company
of Flat Rock, North Carolina, weighed 37,000 pounds and measured 107 feet across.

932
Chocolate Heart

The world's largest, was designed by Luís Morera and produced by Chocovic of Madrid,
Spain. The heart was commissioned by Match.com, and weighed almost 8 tons.

933
Solid Chocolate Oscar Statuettes

Dusted with gold, created by chef Wolfgang Puck for the Governor's Ball
at the Academy Awards dinner party.

934
The World's Largest Piece of Chocolate

was created by Italy's most famous chocolate maker, Perugina, and was unveiled on October 26, 2003, at Turin, Italy's annual Eurochocolate fair. Fashioned after the popular "Perugina Baci," nut-centered chocolates, the gargantuan chocolate took more than 1,000 hours to make, stood more than 6 1/2 feet high, and weighed 6 tons.

935
The Largest Chocolate Bar

ever produced weighed in at 5,026 pounds; it was manufactured by Elah-Dufour United Food Companies, and exhibited at Eurochocolate in March 2000.

936
The Largest Chocolate Marshmallow Easter Egg

was presented on April 4, 1996, by the Rotary Club of Piet Retief, KwaZulu-Natal, South Africa. Standing just over 25 feet high, the egg weighed 8,968 pounds and was supported by an internal steel frame.

937
The World's Largest Piece of Fudge

according to the Guinness Book of Records, was 8 feet long, 4 feet wide, 4 inches thick, and weighed 660 pounds. The giant treat was made by Calico Cottage of Amityville, New York in March, 1999.

938
Chocolate Wonderbra

created by Godiva, and unveiled at Fashion Week in Milan in 2003.

939
The Largest Box of Chocolates
ever made was a Frango mint chocolates box
weighing 3,226 lbs. created by Marshall Field's,
Chicago, Illinois, on November 14, 2002. The
box contained 90,090 individual chocolates.

Wild and Wacky Chocolate Products

940 Chocolate-dipped fortune cookies

941 Cinnamon-chocolate molded chicken wings with white chocolate dipping sauce

942 Chocolate voodoo dolls

943 Chocolate Statue of Liberty

944 Molded chocolate phones: a great way to sweetly tell someone to call you

945 Chocolate-dipped or chocolate chip granola bars

946 Peppered chocolate sauce

947 Softball-size truffles

948 Goat-cheese truffles

949 White chocolate toothpaste

950 Chocolate-flavored breath spray

951 Chocolate perfume

952 Chocolate shampoo

953 Chocolate soap

954 White chocolate tortellini

955 Chocolate caviar

956 Lobster made of chocolate and filled with pralines

957 Chocolate-dipped potato chips

958 Detailed, 14-inch chocolate Lear jet

959 Chocolate motorcycles

960 Chocolate computer keyboards

961 Chocolate computer mouse

962 Chocolate computer disk

963 Chocolate carpentry tools

964 Chocolate photos

965 Chocolate bags to hold mousse and milkshakes

966 Chocolate chickens

967 Chocolate molded into the shape of luxury items like fur coats and Porsches

968 Chocolate noses (sisters Sandra and Ellen Katzman made them for a plastic surgeon to send to his patients)

More Wild and Wacky Chocolate

969 Deep-Fried Mars Bar
Born in Aberdeen, Scotland, the recipe is simple: dip a Mars Bar in
a batter made of flour, cornstarch, and milk or beer, and deep fry in oil
until golden brown. Mars Bars were the first candy bar to be deep-fried,
but others soon followed.

970 Deep-Fried Chocolate Sandwich
Chocoholics in London were introduced to this waist-busting treat by a
British hotel chain in March 2004. The sandwich, which is dipped in batter
and fried, quickly became the fastest selling dessert on the menu.

971 Banania
The first chocolate flour created by Pierre Francois Lardet, in 1914.

972 Bicerin
An Italian drink containing equal amounts of chocolate, coffee, and cream.

973 Cuba Venchi Chocolate Cigars
with dark nougatine filling, white nougat filling, or dark truffle filling
in a real Cuban-style wooden cigar box.

974 Chocolarte
A network of artists who use chocolate as an artistic medium.

975 Chocolate Fool's Day

An annual fundraising event held in Boston, where the region's leading chocolatiers and pastry chefs offer a broad range of chocolate delights for viewing—and tasting!

976 Dipped in Chocolate

The founding editor of *Chocolatier Magazine* and one of the first inductees to the Chocolate Hall of Fame, Joan Steuer had herself dipped in chocolate for the cover of People Magazine—a process that involved having the chocolate applied with a paintbrush and dried with a hair dryer so it wouldn't crack or lose its shine.

'When I die,' I said to my friend, 'I'm not going to be embalmed. I'm going to be dipped.' 'Milk chocolate or bittersweet?' was her immediate concern. This is the rhetorical response of one chocolate addict to another. We both know the answer: Bittersweet.

—Adrianne Marcus,
  from the introduction to
  The Chocolate Bible

Bumper Stickers and T-Shirts

Chocophiles love their obsession
and they don't care who knows it.

977 I brake for chocolate!

978 If it ain't chocolate, it ain't breakfast!

979 Life is too short NOT to eat chocolate!

980 A chocolate in the mouth is worth two on the plate.

981 Nuts just take up space where chocolate ought to be.

982 I could give up chocolate, but I'm not a quitter.

983 Save the earth—it's the only planet that has chocolate.

984 In the beginning, the Lord created chocolate, and he saw that it was good. Then he separated the light from the dark, and it was better.

985 Everything in moderation—except chocolate.

986 If they don't have chocolate in heaven, I'm not going!

987 Coffee, chocolate, men—some things are better rich.

988 Friends are the chocolate chips in the cookies of life.

989 Chocolate: here today, gone today!

Beautiful Chocolate

990
Philosophy

This maker of fine beauty products knows we love chocolate so much that we want to bathe in it. Philosophy makes a 3-in-1 shampoo, conditioner, and body wash in 3 scrumptious fragrances: White Chocolate Hazelnut Cake, Chocolate Ice Cream, and Chocolate Chip Cookies.

991
Richard Donnelly

Known for his artisanal chocolates, Donnelly also makes a line of chocolate essentials body products, which include Dark Chocolate Massage Oil, Luscious Chocolate Body Bar, Dark Chocolate Lip Balm, and Milk Chocolate Lip Balm.

Death by Chocolate

992

In 1648, the Bishop of Chiapa Real in Mexico disallowed chocolate-drinking in church. Because of this, the women of Chiapa Real poisoned his chocolate!

993

England's Charles II reputedly died from drinking poisoned chocolate given to him by his mistress.

It's not that chocolates are a substitute for love. Love is a substitute for chocolate. Chocolate is, let's face it, far more reliable than a man.

—Miranda Ingram

One Last Piece

—⁂—

994
Noticing that there's an ultra-dark chocolate bar
on the kitchen counter

995
Finding, upon closer inspection, that just one piece
is left in the wrapper

996
Deciding that 11 PM isn't too late for chocolate

997
Confirming that there is another chocolate bar
in the cupboard for tomorrow

998
Settling down in your favorite armchair with
the chocolate and a book

999
Eating the chocolate as slowly as you can

1,000
Going to bed with the taste of chocolate
in your mouth

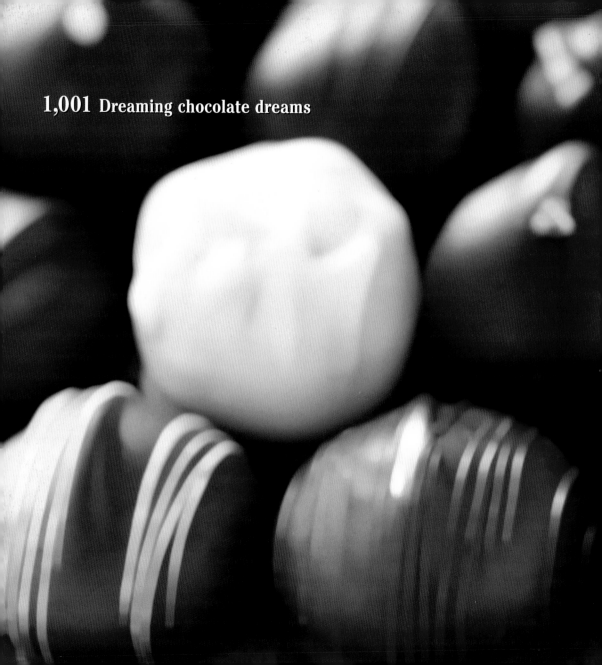

1,001 Dreaming chocolate dreams

Company, www.idahospud.com • Page 132, 137 courtesy of Kraft Foods, Inc., www.kraftfoods.com • Page 44, 99,174-175, 240-241, 242, 248, 257, 266-267, 270-271 courtesy of the Library of Congress, Prints and Photographs Division, www.loc.gov/rr/print/ • Page 254 'Choice Recipes' courtesy of the Rare Book, Manuscript, and Special Collections Library/Duke University/American Memory/Library of Congress, www.memory.loc.gov • Pages 206, 207 courtesy of Li-Lac Chocolates, Inc. NYC • Pages 15, 16-17, 52-53, 54-55,61, 69,130, 243, 246, 247, 275, 279 courtesy of Lindt & Sprüngli AG, www.lindt.com • Pages 115, 208-209 courtesy of MarieBelle, www.mariebelle.com • Page 225 courtesy of Mary Chocolate Co., Ltd., www.mary.co.jp • Pages 154, 155, 282 Photos by Geoffrey Thomas, 188-189 courtesy of Masterfoods USA a division of Mars, Incorporated, ™/® M&M'S, 3 Musketeers, DoveBar, MilkyWay, and Snickers are trademarks of Mars, Incorporated. © Mars, Inc. 2004, www.mars.com • Pages 30-31, 48-49, 60, 93, 106, 107, 134, 169, 214, 252-253 courtesy of Mazet de Montargis, www.mazetconfiseur.com • Page 73 (right inset), 304 courtesy of Moonstruck Chocolate Co., www.moonstruckchocolate.com • Page 102 Photo by Don Shugart, 103 Photo by K.C. Montgomery, courtesy of Myers Horse Farms, Inc., www.ZipsChocolateChip.com • Page 19 courtesy of National Confectioners Association, www.CandyUSA.org • Page 76, 77 courtesy of Jimmy Nelson and Farfel • Page 68, 70, 71, 72, 73 (left inset), 80, 111, 166-167 courtesy of Nestlé USA, www.nestleusa.com • Page 156 Photo by Sandy Nicholson, www.sandynicholson.com • Pages 178, 179 Nutella images, courtesy of Ferrero U.S.A. Inc., www.nutellausa.com • Page 121 Photo by Zeva Oelbaum, www.zevaphoto.com • Page 211 'Louvre' Photo by Philippe Houze, courtesy of Francois Payard of Payard Patisserie & Bistro in New York, NY, and Manhasset, NY, www.payard.com • Page 310 courtesy of Philosophy, www.philosophy.com • Pages 24-25, 146-147, 286-287 courtesy of Photofest, www.photofestnyc.com • Pages 64, 116, 171 (inset) courtesy of Popperfoto/retrofile, www.retrofile.com • Page 148, 217, 280-281, courtesy of Recchiuti Confections, www.recchuiticonfections.com • Page 23, 67, 79, 191, 254 (photo inset), 285 courtesy of retrofile.com, www.retrofile.com • Page 277 Rocher image, courtesy of Ferrero U.S.A., Inc., www.rocherusa.com • Pages 20-21, 182-183, 185, 210 courtesy of Russell Stover Candies, www.russellstover.com • Page 47, 220, 221 (Illustration by Robert Hullinger) courtesy of Scharffen Berger Chocolate Maker, Inc., www.scharffenberger.com • Page 158 'Frozen Hot Chocolate' (inset) courtesy of Serendipity 3, www.serendipity3.com • Pages 222, 223 courtesy of Sterling Truffle Bar, www.sterlingtrufflebar.com • Pages 66, 192-193 courtesy Michael Stefanos • Page 119 courtesy of Sugar/a dessert bar, Photo by Steinkamp & Ballogg Photography • Page 4 Photo by Eleanor Thompson, www.EleanorThompson.com • Page 308 Photo by Mary Tiegreen • Page 157 Courtesy of Kraft Foods, www.toblerone.com • Page 187 TootsiePop/Tootsie Rolls, courtesy of Tootsie Roll Industries, Inc., www.tootsie.com • Page 245 Photo by Jennifer Roper, courtesy of Teuscher USA, www.teuscherusa.com • Page 56, 131, 140, 170, 260 Photos by John Uher, www.johnuher.com • Page 293 UPS: This image is reproduced with permission of United Parcel Servcice of America, Inc. © 2004 United Parcel Service of America, Inc. All rights reserved. www.ups.com • Page 100-101 Photo by © 2004/Jack Vartoogian/Front Row Photos • Page 294 courtesy of Victorian Chocolate Molds, www.victorianchocolatemolds.com • Page 117, 184, 196-197 courtesy of Whitman's Candies, www.russellstover.com

Kahlua is a trademark of Allied Domecq Spirits USA

Crayola is a trademark of Binney & Smith

Cadbury is a trademark of Cadbury Trebor Bassett

Mini Milano is a trademark of Campbell Soup Company

Chipwich is a trademark of Chipwich, Inc.

Buster Bar and Dilly Bar are trademarks of Dairy Queen

Nutella is a trademark of Ferrero USA, Inc.

Cocoa Puffs is a trademark of General Mills, Inc.

All Abouts, Samoas, Tagalongs, and Thin Mints are trademarks of Girl Scouts of the USA

Klondike Bar is a trademark of Good Humor-Breyers

5th Avenue, Almond Joy, Heath Bar Crunch, Hershey's Hugs, Hershey's Kisses, Hershey's Syrup, Kit Kat, Mallo Cup, Milk Duds, Mounds, Mr. Goodbar, Oh Henry!, Reese's Peanut Butter Cups, Reese's Pieces, Rolo, Whoppers, and York Peppermint Patties are trademarks of Hershey Foods Corporation

Idaho Spud Bar is a trademark of Idaho Candy Company

Cocoa Krispies, Krave Bar, and Pop Tart are trademarks of Kellogg Company

Baker's Chocolate, Cocoa Pebbles, Oreo, and Toblerone are trademarks of Kraft Foods, Inc.

Dove Bars, Dove Bites, Dove Promises, Ethel M, M&Ms, Milky Way, Snickers, Three Musketeers, and Twix are trademarks of Mars, Incorporated and its affiliates.

Frango is a trademark of Marshall Field's, a division of Target, Inc.

100 Grand, Baby Ruth, Baci Chocolates, Buncha Crunch, Butterfinger Bar, Chunky, Crunch, Ethel M, Goobers, Quik, Raisinets, Sno-Caps, and Toll House are trademarks of Nestlé USA

Necco is a trademark of New England Confectionery Company

Twin Bing is a trademark of Palmer Candy Company

Valomilk is a trademark of Russell Sifers Candy Company

Whitman's Sampler is a trademark of Whitman's Candies, Inc.

Goo Goo Cluster is a trademark of Standard Candy Company

Frappuccino is a trademark of Starbucks Corporation

Andes, Charleston Chew, Junior Mints, and Tootsie Roll are trademarks of Tootsie Roll Industries

Slim-Fast is a trademark of Unilever Best Foods affiliated companies.